ILLUSTRATED LIBRARY OF COOKING

VOLUME **10** Hot-Lan

Hotdog fancier? Awed by your supermarket's array of instants and mixes and wondering how to use them creatively? Love to cook for others, to bake your Christmas gifts? Like to put up pickles and preserves, to make jams and jellies? Then you'll find Volume 10 (it is four books in one) written just for you. It's jam-packed with cooking tips and gift ideas.

ROCKVILLE HOUSE PUBLISHERS, INC.
ROCKVILLE CENTRE, NEW YORK 11570

Family Circle®

Illustrated Library of

COOKING

YOUR READY REFERENCE FOR A LIFETIME OF GOOD EATING

Picture Credits:

The Advisory Council for Jams, Jellies and Preserves • American Spice Trade Association • Best Foods, a Division of CPC International • Breakstone Foods • General Mills • National Live Stock and Meat Board • George Nordhausen • Pacific Kitchen • Pepperidge Farm • Pickle Packers International

Salmon Salad Tart

Table of Contents

1158

One of the best of all ways to serve frankfurters is in *Summer Grill*, a glistening mixture of franks, lamb patties, tomato slices and pineapple chunks sautéed separately but served together with a zippy mustard.

HOTDOG

HAPPENINGS

HOTDOG HAPPENINGS:
NEW WAYS WITH AN OLD FAVORITE

Although we think of hotdogs as being as American as baseball, they aren't. They're a German sausage, probably from the region of Frankfurt, hence the name, frankfurter.

Nearly everyone likes hotdogs. A good thing, too, because they are both economical and adaptable. The favorite way to eat them, of course, is in hotdog buns with all the trimmings, preferably outdoors at a baseball game. But they are equally good in skillet dinners and casseroles. They team well with many vegetables—particularly with cabbage and kraut, beans and potatoes. They also wear many sauces well:

sweet-sour glazes, barbecue, chili and mustard sauces. The mini variety, cocktail sausages, are party perfect because they're bite-size and easy to manage with a toothpick.

A plump cousin of the hotdog—and one that can be used very much like it—is *knackwurst,* an old German favorite. Like many hotdogs, it's made of finely chopped pork and beef; the seasonings are similar, too, except that knackwurst contains a touch more garlic.

In the recipes that follow, you'll find dozens of new ways to serve hotdogs as well as a number of old favorites.

• • •

TIPS ON BUYING HOTDOGS:

Take your pick of those made with pork and beef or veal or, if you prefer, with beef only. All are seasoned with salt and a variety of spices, then smoked. They may be skinless or in natural casings. Sizes range from the jumbo fat links to the cocktail-size bites. Although all are ready-to-eat (in days past they weren't and had to be cooked carefully and thoroughly), most people prefer their hotdogs hot. A quick heating in boiling water is all that's needed to bring out their best flavor.

It's a good idea to buy hotdogs by brand

names—they're your key to quality. Each manufacturer has his own recipe for making his product, thus flavors will vary somewhat from brand to brand. Try several, then pick the one that your family likes best.

HOW MANY HOT DOGS PER PERSON?

Two for big eaters, one for those with more delicate appetites. Generally speaking, one pound of hotdogs will serve 4 to 6 persons, somewhat more if mixed into casseroles or extended in skillet dinners.

SOME RECIPES
THAT "PUT ON THE DOG"

Summer Grill
One after the other, meats, pineapple and to-matoes go into skillets. If you have a griddle, you can speed the preparation even more.
Makes 8 servings

    8 slices bacon
    1 pound ground lamb
    1 tablespoon chopped fresh mint or 1 tea-spoon mint flakes, crumbled
    1 teaspoon salt
    ⅛ teaspoon pepper
    16 frankfurters
    6 tablespoons (¾ stick) butter or margarine
    8 slices pineapple (from a 1-pound can), well drained
    4 medium-size tomatoes, halved crosswise

1 Sauté bacon until fat starts to cook out in a medium-size frying pan; remove and drain for next step.
2 Combine lamb, mint, salt and pepper in a medium-size bowl; mix lightly until well blended. Shape into 8 patties about ½ inch thick. Wrap a bacon slice around each; fasten with a wood-en pick.
3 Sauté patties, turning once, in bacon drip-pings in frying pan 15 minutes, or until lamb is done as you like it; keep warm.
4 Score frankfurters diagonally about ¼ inch deep; sauté, turning several times, in 2 table-spoons of the butter or margarine in a large frying pan 10 minutes, or until lightly browned.
5 Brown pineapple slices, turning once, in 2 tablespoons of the remaining butter or marga-rine in a second large frying pan; push to one side. Add remaining butter or margarine and tomato halves, flat side down, to same pan; heat slowly until tomatoes are hot.
6 Stack frankfurters in the center of a large serving platter; arrange lamb patties, pineapple slices and tomato halves around edge. Garnish with watercress and serve with prepared mus-tard, if you wish.

Hotdog Hoedown
The party is off to a lot of fun when everyone master-chefs his own sandwich.

Count on at least 2 frankfurters and 1 split and buttered hamburger bun for each serving. Set them out near the grill; place glazing sauces

with brushes in separate saucepans on side of grill. *(Recipe for* GINGER-MOLASSES GLAZE, HON-EY-MUSTARD GLAZE, *and* TOMATO TOPPING GLAZE *follow.)* For grilling, make a double frank, hold-ing 2 together with 2 short metal meat skewers. (Use tongs for turning.) Or thread several franks crosswise onto 2 long skewers, and guests can "divvy up." Brush the frankfurters with your sauce choice, then grill over hot coals, turning often and brushing with more sauce, 5 to 10 minutes, or until heated through and richly glazed. (Time will depend on how hot coals are and distance of franks from coals.) Toast buns alongside franks on grill, then butter, if you wish. Pop each 2 franks into a bun; top with your choice of extras—prepared mustard, catsup, chili sauce, sweet-onion rings, pickle relish or shredded cheese.

Ginger-Molasses Glaze
It's mildly spiced with a Far East flavor.
Makes 1 cup

    ¼ cup molasses
    ¼ cup ginger marmalade
    ¼ cup prepared mustard
    ¼ cup vinegar
    ¼ teaspoon curry powder

Combine all ingredients in a small saucepan; heat slowly until bubbly-hot.

Tomato Topping Glaze
It's real peppy, and doubles for both glaze and topping.
Makes 3 cups

    1 large onion, chopped (1 cup)
    4 tablespoons (½ stick) butter or margarine
    2 cans (8 ounces each) tomato sauce
    1 teaspoon salt
    3 tablespoons cider vinegar
    2 tablespoons corn syrup
    ½ cup chopped celery
    ¼ cup finely chopped celery leaves
    1 teaspoon leaf basil, crumbled

Sauté onion until soft in butter or margarine in a medium-size saucepan; stir in remaining in-gredients. Simmer 15 minutes to blend flavors.

Honey-Mustard Glaze
Tart, sweet, and spicy—and thick enough to make a sparkling glaze.
Makes about 1 cup

    ½ cup sugar

Hotdogs needn't simply be served in hotdog buns. Try slitting them and stuffing with tasty herbs, or slicing crosswise or slashing and bending into circles.

Another excellent way to serve franks is as kebabs. Skewer together with green olives or for a Hawaiian touch, with fresh, frozen or canned pineapple cubes.

2 teaspoons dry mustard
¼ teaspoon ground cloves
½ cup honey
½ cup vinegar
2 tablespoons vegetable oil

Combine all ingredients in a small saucepan. Simmer, stirring often, 10 minutes, or until slightly thick.

Frankfurter Fiesta

An all-American outdoor favorite richly glazed with a spicy-sweet sauce.
Makes 4 servings

1 small onion, chopped (¼ cup)
1 tablespoon butter or margarine
1 teaspoon chili powder
8 frankfurters (about 1 pound)
½ cup catsup
¼ cup water
1 tablespoon brown sugar
1 tablespoon cider vinegar
½ teaspoon seasoned salt
½ teaspoon Worcestershire sauce

1 Sauté onion in butter or margarine until golden in large frying pan; stir in chili powder; cook 1 minute longer.
2 Place frankfurters in single layer in frying pan, turning to coat with seasoned-onion mixture.
3 Mix remaining ingredients in a 1-cup measure; pour over frankfurters.
4 Cover; simmer over hot coals 10 minutes, or until frankfurters are puffed and heated through.

Hotdog Hots

String them on long skewers, then "divvy up" and eat with chunks of sour-dough bread.
Makes 8 servings

4 slices bacon
8 frankfurters (about 1 pound)
8 pickled yellow wax peppers
  Bottled barbecue sauce

1 Halve bacon, then fry slowly in medium-size frying pan just until fat starts to cook out; drain on paper toweling. (Bacon cooks crisper on grill if started this way.)
2 Wrap a half slice around each frankfurter; thread alternately with peppers onto long skewers; brush with barbecue sauce.

3 Grill over hot coals, turning and brushing often with sauce, 10 minutes, or until frankfurters are richly glazed and peppers are heated through.

Hotdog Saucies

Franks simmer in a mildly spiced tomato sauce, with plenty left to spoon over rolls.
Makes 8 servings

1 medium-size onion, chopped (½ cup)
¼ cup vegetable oil
2 cans (10¾ ounces) condensed tomato soup
1 cup sliced celery
¼ cup firmly packed brown sugar
2 teaspoons leaf oregano, crumbled
1 bay leaf
1 cup water
2 tablespoons cider vinegar
1 teaspoon Worcestershire sauce
2 pounds frankfurters (about 16)
8 split frankfurter rolls

1 Sauté onion in vegetable oil just until soft in large frying pan; stir in soup, celery, brown sugar, oregano, bay leaf, water, vinegar and Worcestershire sauce; heat to boiling.
2 Score frankfurters almost through every ½ inch; place in sauce; cover.
3 Cook over hot coals (or over medium heat of kitchen range) 15 minutes, or until heated through. Remove bay leaf.
4 Toast rolls, then butter, if you wish. Spoon frankfurters and sauce over.

Hotdog Winders

Wrap partially cooked strips of bacon around hot dogs, then grill until they sizzle.
Makes 8 servings

8 slices bacon
8 frankfurters (about 1 pound)
8 frankfurter rolls, buttered
1 jar (1 quart) pickled sweet red peppers
1 package (½ pound) unsliced process American cheese, cut in 1-inch cubes

1 Fry bacon slowly just until fat begins to cook out in large heavy frying pan; drain on paper toweling.
2 Wrap a slice around each frankfurter; fasten with wooden picks.
3 Let everyone grill his frankfurter and toast the roll to his own liking. Serve cheese cubes and peppers separately to munch on.

Pickle Pups

Stuff hotdogs with a strip of dill pickle and glaze with ready-to-go meat sauce—they're that simple.
Makes 8 servings, 2 hotdogs each

16 frankfurters
 1 large dill pickle, cut into 16 thin strips
    Bottled steak sauce
16 split frankfurter rolls, toasted

1 Slit each frankfurter lengthwise; stuff with a pickle strip; fasten with wooden picks. Place on grill about 6 inches above hot coals.
2 Grill, turning and brushing often with steak sauce, 10 minutes, or until crispy-brown. Serve in toasted frankfurter rolls with prepared mustard or catsup, if you wish.

Italian Beanies

Seasoned green beans go inside and sliced salami and mushroom sauce on the outside.
Makes 8 servings, 2 hotdogs each

 1 can (1 pound) whole Blue Lake green beans, drained
¼ cup bottled oil-and-vinegar dressing
 1 can (about 11 ounces) mushroom gravy
¼ cup catsup
 1 tablespoon prepared horseradish
16 frankfurters
 2 packages (8 ounces each) sliced large salami
16 split frankfurter rolls, toasted

1 Place beans in a pie plate; drizzle with oil-and-vinegar dressing; let stand 30 minutes to season.
2 Heat mushroom gravy with catsup to boiling in a small saucepan; stir in horseradish; remove from heat.
3 Slit each frankfurter lengthwise; stuff with 3 beans. Wrap a slice of salami around each; fasten with wooden picks. Place on grill about 6 inches above hot coals.
4 Grill, turning and brushing often with mushroom sauce, 10 minutes, or until crispy-brown. Serve in toasted frankfurter rolls.

Trade-Winds Treasure Dogs

Bacon, bananas and curry sauce are the flavor dress-ups. For the "treasure," choose green-tip fruit.
Makes 8 servings, 2 hotdogs each

 4 tablespoons (½ stick) butter or margarine
 2 teaspoons curry powder
 2 tablespoons all-purpose flour
1½ cups water
 1 envelope instant beef broth
    OR: 1 beef-flavor bouillon cube
 2 bananas
16 frankfurters
16 slices bacon (about 1 pound)
16 split frankfurter rolls, toasted

1 Melt butter or margarine in a small saucepan; stir in curry powder; cook 2 minutes.
2 Blend in flour, then stir in water and beef broth or bouillon cube, crushing bouillon cube, if using, with a spoon. Cook, stirring constantly, until sauce thickens and boils 1 minute; remove from heat.
3 Halve bananas crosswise, then quarter each half. Slit each frankfurter lengthwise; stuff with a strip of banana. Wrap each with a bacon slice; fasten with wooden picks. Place on grill about 6 inches above hot coals.
4 Grill, turning and brushing often with curry sauce, 20 minutes, or until bacon is crisp. Serve in toasted frankfurter rolls.

Frankly Hot Kebabs
Makes 8 servings

16 small white onions, peeled
 1 large green pepper, cut in 16 squares
 8 frankfurters (about 1 pound), cut in half
16 pineapple chunks (from a 14-ounce can)
    PEPPY BARBECUE SAUCE (recipe follows)
 8 frankfurter rolls
    Melted butter or margarine
    Sesame seeds

1 Cook onions in boiling salted water in medium-size saucepan 5 minutes; add green-pepper squares; cook 3 minutes longer, or just until onions are tender-crisp; drain.
2 String 8 small skewers with alternate pieces of frankfurter, pineapple, green pepper and onion; place on foil-covered broiler pan (or on an outdoor grill, if you wish); brush with PEPPY BARBECUE SAUCE.
3 Broil, with top of food 4 inches from heat, turning often and brushing with sauce, 10 minutes, or until heated through.
4 While kebabs grill, brush rolls with melted butter or margarine; sprinkle tops with sesame seeds; heat in oven (if broiling indoors) or on outdoor grill.
5 To serve, place a kebab in roll; pull out skewer.

PEPPY BARBECUE SAUCE—Blend ½ cup catsup, 3 tablespoons prepared mustard, 3 tablespoons

molasses, 3 tablespoons cider vinegar, 1 teaspoon grated onion and ⅛ teaspoon liquid red pepper seasoning in small screw-top jar or bowl. Makes 1 cup.

●

Fancy Frank Kebabs
Makes 6 servings

6 frankfurters, halved
6 slices bacon, halved
6 thick slices mild onion
3 green peppers, quartered
3 tomatoes, quartered
6 fresh or canned mushrooms
 MUSTARD GLAZE (recipe follows)
6 buttered, toasted, split large rolls

1 Wrap halved frankfurters with bacon; fasten with wooden picks.
2 Thread each of 6 greased skewers with an onion slice, then alternate pieces of frankfurter, green pepper and tomato; end with a mushroom; brush with MUSTARD GLAZE.
3 Place on grill over glowing coals; cook, turning often and brushing with sauce, 10 to 15 minutes, or until bacon is crisp.
4 Remove picks; slide kebab onto roll.
 MUSTARD GLAZE— Simmer ½ cup sugar, 2 teaspoons dry mustard, ¼ teaspoon ground cloves, ½ cup honey, ½ cup cider vinegar and 2 tablespoons vegetable oil 10 minutes, or until syrupy. Makes about 1 cup.

Barbecued Franks-In-a-Bun
Wieners simmer in a spicy hot sauce that makes the topping, too.
Makes 6 servings

1 medium-size onion, chopped (½ cup)
2 tablespoons butter or margarine
2 cans (8 ounces each) tomato sauce
1 tablespoon molasses
1 tablespoon cider vinegar
1 tablespoon prepared mustard
½ teaspoon salt
½ teaspoon leaf basil, crumbled
12 frankfurters (about 1½ pounds)
12 split frankfurter rolls, toasted and buttered

1 Sauté onion in butter or margarine just until soft in large frying pan. Stir in tomato sauce, molasses, vinegar, mustard, salt and basil; simmer, uncovered, 5 minutes.

2 Arrange frankfurters in sauce; cover; simmer 10 minutes, or until puffed and bubbly-hot.
3 Place frankfurters in rolls; spoon sauce over.

●

Wiener Winners
Makes 8 servings

8 thin slices of mild onion, halved
8 thin slices of tomato, halved
 Butter or margarine
 Sugar
8 frankfurters (about 1 pound)
⅓ cup pickle relish
¼ cup bottled thin French dressing
1 jar (8 ounces) soft process cheese spread
8 frankfurter rolls, split and buttered

1 Place onion and tomato slices on foil-covered broiler pan; dot with butter or margarine; sprinkle lightly with sugar.
2 Cut frankfurters lengthwise almost through; fill with relish; brush with French dressing; place on broiler pan.
3 Broil, with top of food 4 inches from heat, brushing frankfurters several times with French dressing to keep from charring, 10 minutes, or until heated through.
4 While frankfurters heat, spoon soft cheese spread into top of double boiler; heat over simmering water.
5 Slide foil with food from pan; toast buttered rolls quickly.
6 Tuck a stuffed frankfurter and 2 onion-topped tomato slices into each roll; dribble hot cheese spread over top. Keep seconds hot in a warm oven.

●

Franks Diable
No extra spread needed here, as hotdogs are filled with creamy egg salad.
Makes 8 servings, 2 hotdogs each

8 hard-cooked eggs, shelled and chopped
4 tablespoons chopped ripe olives
½ cup mayonnaise or salad dressing
2 tablespoons prepared mustard
1 teaspoon salt
2 drops liquid red pepper seasoning
16 frankfurters
3 packages (6 ounces each) minced ham
16 split frankfurter rolls, toasted

1 Combine eggs and olives in a medium-size bowl. Blend mayonnaise or salad dressing, mustard, salt and liquid red pepper seasoning in a 1-cup measure; fold into the egg mixture.
2 Slit each frankfurter lengthwise; stuff with about 3 tablespoons egg mixture. Wrap a slice

Bound to be a hit at any picnic with both young and old alike, spicy, tomatoey Barbecued Franks-In-a-Bun.

Beautiful variation on the hotdog theme: Hawaiian Windups, with frankfurters and pineapple spears in ham.

1166

of minced ham around each; fasten with wooden picks. Place on grill about 6 inches above hot coals.
3 Grill, turning often, 10 minutes, or until crispy-brown. Serve in toasted frankfurter rolls.

●

Bologna-and-Swiss Hotdogs
This twosome stars again, with cheese as the filling and ham-bologna as the wrapper.
Makes 8 servings, 2 hotdogs each

1 package (8 ounces) sliced process Swiss cheese
16 slices bologna (from 3 six-ounce packages)
16 frankfurters
16 split frankfurter rolls, toasted

1 Cut cheese slices in 4 strips each; halve bologna diagonally.
2 Slit each frankfurter lengthwise; stuff with 2 strips of cheese. Wrap 2 half slices bologna around each; fasten with wooden picks. Place on grill about 6 inches above hot coals.

3 Grill, turning often, 10 minutes, or until crispy-brown and cheese melts. Serve in toasted frankfurter rolls.

Frankfurter-Salad Buns
Pile toasty rolls with creamy coleslaw, pop a sautéed hotdog on top, and they're ready.
Makes 4 servings

    4 frankfurters (about ½ pound)
    4 tablespoons (½ stick) butter or margarine
    4 split frankfurter rolls, toasted
    1 tablespoon prepared mustard
    2 cups (1-pound container) coleslaw

1 Score frankfurters; sauté in half the butter or margarine just until hot.
2 Spread toasted rolls with remaining butter or margarine and mustard; fill with coleslaw, then top each with a frankfurter. Garnish with sliced sweet yellow wax pepper, if you wish.

Polynesian Franks
Sauce is lightly spiced to please a youngster's taste.
Makes 8 servings

    1 large onion, chopped (1 cup)
    3 tablespoons vegetable oil
    2 tablespoons cornstarch
    1 tablespoon curry powder
    ¼ teaspoon ground allspice
    1 teaspoon salt
    1 can (about 1 pound, 5 ounces) crushed
      pineapple
    2 tablespoons cider vinegar
    12 frankfurters, cut diagonally into 1-inch
       lengths
       SESAME BUNS (recipe follows)

1 Sauté onion in vegetable oil until soft in a large frying pan.
2 Mix cornstarch, curry powder, allspice and salt in a cup; stir into onion mixture; cook, stirring constantly, just until bubbly.
3 Stir in pineapple and syrup and vinegar; cook over low heat, stirring constantly, until sauce mixture thickens and boils 3 minutes.
4 Place frankfurter pieces in sauce; heat to boiling; cover. Simmer 15 minutes, or until heated through.
5 Serve as is, or spoon over SESAME BUNS.
   SESAME BUNS—Place 1 tablespoon sesame seeds in a small frying pan; heat slowly, shaking pan constantly, 3 to 5 minutes, or until toasty-golden. Toast 8 split frankfurter rolls or 8 hamburger buns; brush with 4 tablespoons (½ stick)

melted butter or margarine; sprinkle with sesame seeds.

Pickaback Biscuits
Simply cut biscuits, doughnut style; tuck a half hotdog into each and bake.
Bake at 450° for 10 minutes. Makes 6 to 8 servings

    2 packages refrigerated plain or buttermilk
      biscuits
    10 frankfurters, halved crosswise
    1 can (10½ ounces) condensed cream of cel-
      ery soup
    1 can (8 ounces) tomato sauce

1 Separate biscuits. Cut a ½-inch round from center of each with a cookie cutter or center of a doughnut cutter. Place large rounds, 2 inches apart, on a lightly greased cookie sheet.
2 Place a frankfurter half in each hole; press a small round at edge of each biscuit to decorate, or bake separately for nibbles.
3 Bake in very hot oven (450°) 10 minutes, or until biscuits are golden.
4 While biscuits bake, combine soup with tomato sauce in a small saucepan; heat, stirring several times, to boiling.
5 Place biscuits on a large serving platter; serve sauce separately.

Hawaiian Windups
Sweet-sour sauce glazes pineapple-stuffed franks wrapped with ham.
Makes 8 servings, 2 hotdogs each

    ½ cup firmly packed brown sugar
    2 tablespoons cornstarch
    1 cup water
    ½ cup cider vinegar
    ½ cup (1 stick) butter or margarine
    16 frankfurters
    1 can (about 1 pound, 5 ounces) pineapple
      spears, drained
    1 package (8 ounces) sliced boiled ham
    16 split frankfurter rolls, toasted
       TRIPLE OLIVE STICKS (recipe follows)

1 Mix brown sugar and cornstarch in a medium-size saucepan; stir in water and vinegar.

1167

Cook, stirring constantly, until sauce thickens and boils 3 minutes; remove from heat. Stir in butter or margarine until melted.

2 Slit each frankfurter lengthwise; stuff with a pineapple spear. Cut each ham slice into 4 strips; wrap 2 strips around each frankfurter; fasten with wooden picks. Place on grill about 6 inches above hot coals.

3 Grill, turning and brushing often with sauce, 10 minutes, or until crispy-brown. Serve in toasted frankfurter rolls with TRIPLE OLIVE STICKS; garnish rolls with watercress, if you wish.

TRIPLE OLIVE STICKS—Pare 2 medium-size carrots; cut lengthwise into thin sticks. Place in a bowl of ice and water to chill and crisp. Just before serving, drain; thread 2 sticks through each of 3 pitted ripe olives.

Double Porkers

Buy the new tiny smoked sausages in packages for the zesty-flavor filling.
Makes 8 servings, 2 hotdogs each

    2 cans (8 ounces each) tomato sauce
    1 teaspoon Italian seasoning
    ¼ cup sweet-pickle relish
   16 frankfurters
    2 packages (5 ounces each) smoked cocktail
      sausages
   16 split frankfurter rolls, toasted

1 Combine tomato sauce and Italian seasoning in a small saucepan. Heat to boiling, then simmer 2 minutes; stir in pickle relish; remove from heat.

2 Slit each frankfurter lengthwise; stuff with 2 cocktail sausages; fasten with wooden picks. Place on grill about 6 inches above hot coals.

3 Grill, turning and brushing often with tomato sauce, 10 minutes, or until crispy-brown. Serve in toasted frankfurter rolls.

Glazed Knackwurst

Husky-size smoked franks simmer to spicy goodness in a snappy sweet-sour sauce.
Makes 8 servings

    1 medium-size onion, chopped (½ cup)
    2 tablespoons butter or margarine
    ¼ cup sugar
    1 teaspoon dry mustard
    ⅛ teaspoon ground cloves
    ¼ cup honey

1168

    ¼ cup cider vinegar
    8 knackwursts (about 2 pounds)

1 Sauté onion in butter or margarine until golden in medium-size frying pan; remove pan from heat; stir in sugar, mustard, cloves, honey and vinegar.

2 Coat knackwursts with sauce in pan, arranging them in a single layer. Simmer, covered, turning once or twice, 10 minutes, or until puffed and glazed.

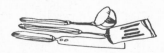

Spicy Hotdogs

Hotdogs simmer in a spicy sweet-sour sauce to enjoy as is or in crusty rolls.
Makes 4 servings

    1 small onion, chopped (¼ cup)
    1 tablespoon butter or margarine
    1 teaspoon chili powder
    8 frankfurters
    ½ cup catsup
    ¼ cup water
    1 tablespoon brown sugar
    1 tablespoon cider vinegar
    ½ teaspoon seasoned salt
    ½ teaspoon Worcestershire sauce

1 Sauté onion in butter or margarine until soft in a large frying pan; stir in chili powder; cook 1 minute longer.

2 Score frankfurters diagonally about ¼ inch deep; place in a single layer in frying pan, turning to coat well with onion mixture.

3 Mix catsup, water, brown sugar, vinegar, seasoned salt and Worcestershire sauce in a 1-cup measure; pour over frankfurters. Heat to boiling; cover.

4 Simmer 10 minutes, or until frankfurters are puffed and heated through.

Hotdog Jambalaya

This version of a Southern specialty goes from skillet to table in about 40 minutes.
Makes 6 servings

    8 frankfurters, sliced ½ inch thick
   1½ cups uncooked rice
    2 tablespoons butter or margarine
    2 cans (about 1 pound each) stewed toma-
      toes
   1½ cups water
   1½ teaspoons garlic salt
    2 cans (5 ounces each) boned turkey, diced
    ¼ cup diced green pepper

1 Sauté frankfurters and rice in butter or margarine in a large frying pan, stirring often, until rice is golden.
2 Stir in tomatoes, water and garlic salt; place turkey on top; cover.
3 Simmer, stirring once, 30 minutes, or until rice is tender and liquid is absorbed.
4 Spoon into a serving bowl; sprinkle with green pepper.

Franks Romanoff

This heat-and-serve meat and noodles packaged with their own sour-cream sauce mix are your speedy helpers.
Makes 4 servings

1 package noodles with sour-cream-cheese-sauce mix
2 cups thinly sliced celery
8 frankfurters
4 tablespoons (½ stick) butter or margarine
½ cup milk
Chopped parsley

1 Combine noodles and celery in a large saucepan; cook, following label directions. Drain; return to saucepan.
2 While noodles cook, halve frankfurters lengthwise, then crosswise. Sauté in 2 tablespoons of the butter or margarine until lightly browned in a medium-size frying pan.
3 Stir remaining 2 tablespoons butter or margarine, milk and sauce mix from package into noodles; spoon into a serving bowl. Arrange frankfurters in a pretty pattern on top; sprinkle with chopped parsley.

Jiffy Boiled Dinner

Wieners, three canned vegetables, and fresh cabbage make this inviting platter meal.
Makes 4 servings

1 can (about 1 pound) sliced carrots
1 can (about 1 pound) white potatoes, drained
8 frankfurters
1 small cabbage (about 1½ pounds) trimmed, quartered and cored
½ teaspoon salt
1 can (about 1 pound) small whole beets
¼ teaspoon dillweed
Pepper

1 Place carrots and liquid in a kettle or Dutch oven; add potatoes in a mound at one side.
2 Score frankfurters diagonally about ¼ inch deep; add to kettle; lay cabbage wedges on top of meat and vegetables; sprinkle all with salt. Heat to boiling; cover. Simmer 15 minutes, or until cabbage is crisply tender.
3 Heat beets in liquid to boiling in a small saucepan; drain.
4 Place cabbage wedges, frankfurters, potatoes, carrots and beets in separate mounds on a large serving platter; sprinkle with dillweed and pepper. Serve with prepared horseradish, if you wish.

Spritely to look at, savory to eat: hotdog chunks on a bed of sauerkraut spoked with pineapple and peppers.

HOT DOG HAPPENINGS

Wieners and Kraut
Canned apples and sausages add the continental flavor dress-ups.
Makes 4 servings

1 can (1 pound, 11 ounces) sauerkraut, drained
1 can (about 1 pound) pie-sliced apples
1 clove garlic, minced
⅛ teaspoon pepper
1 cup apple juice
4 frankfurters
1 packages (8 ounces) heat-and-serve sausages

1 Combine sauerkraut, apples and liquid, garlic, pepper and apple juice in a large frying pan; toss lightly to mix; cover. Simmer, stirring once or twice, 30 minutes to blend flavors.
2 Score frankfurters diagonally about ¼ inch deep; place frankfurters and sausages over sauerkraut mixture; cover again. Simmer 15 minutes, or until meats are hot.
3 Arrange frankfurters and sausages, alternately, around edge of a large serving platter; spoon sauerkraut mixture in center.

Skillet Franks and Sauerkraut
Makes 4 servings

6 strips of bacon, diced
1 small onion, sliced
1 can (1 pound, 14 ounces) sauerkraut, drained
1 cup apple juice
1 tablespoon brown sugar
1 teaspoon caraway seeds
1 medium-size red-skinned apple
6 frankfurters

1 Heat bacon in large frying pan until fat begins to melt; push bacon to one side; cook onion 2 to 3 minutes; add sauerkraut; cook 5 minutes.
2 Stir in apple juice, sugar and caraway seeds; grate in half the apple; cover; simmer 30 minutes. (Save rest of apple for garnish.)
3 Place frankfurters on top; cover; simmer 15 minutes, or until frankfurters are heated through; garnish with rest of apple cut into wedges.

Crown Wiener-Sauerkraut Roast
Just see how franks and sauerkraut put on the dog here!
Makes 8 servings

1 large onion, chopped (1 cup)
4 tablespoons (½ stick) butter or margarine
1 apple, pared, quartered, cored and diced
1 can (1 pound, 11 ounces) sauerkraut, drained and chopped
4 cups slightly dry bread cubes (8 slices)
1 teaspoon salt
½ teaspoon leaf thyme, crumbled
½ teaspoon dry mustard
¼ teaspoon caraway seeds
Dash of pepper
1 egg, slightly beaten
2 pounds frankfurters (about 16)

1 Sauté onion in butter or margarine just until soft in large frying pan; stir in apple; cook 1 minute longer; remove from heat.
2 Stir in sauerkraut, bread cubes, salt, thyme, mustard, caraway seeds and pepper. Drizzle egg over; toss lightly to mix.
3 To shape roast: Line a deep saucepan or bowl, about 6 inches in diameter, with a sheet of heavy foil big enough to cover bottom and side with a 3-inch overhang. Stand frankfurters around side. (They will extend about 2 inches above top of pan or bowl.) Spoon sauerkraut mixture into center.
4 Strip corn husks into ribbons, then tie several together to form a rope. Tie around frankfurters as close as possible to rim of pan or bowl. (No corn husks? Tie franks with string.)
5 Place a second sheet of foil over top of frankfurters; seal to the 3-inch overhang of bottom sheet with a triple fold so roast is sealed completely.
6 Lift "package" carefully from pan or bowl; set in a kettle. Pour in boiling water to half the depth of package.
7 Cook, uncovered, on grill over hot coals (or over medium heat of kitchen range) 1 hour, or until piping hot. (Keep water boiling during entire cooking time, adding more as needed.)
8 Remove kettle from grill. Lift foil package from kettle, protecting hands with pot holders; let drain; place on serving board. Slit foil around bottom with scissors. (Have paper toweling handy to catch any juices that may seep out.) Lift off foil cover.
9 To serve, spoon stuffing from center, then pull frankfurters out with a fork, leaving husks or string in place. Serve plain or with mustard and pickle relish.

Sensational way to serve frankfurters—picket-fencing in a mountain of nippy stuffing. The Wiener Tiara Bake recipe below tells you how—and it's easier than you suspect!

Wiener Tiara Bake

Frankfurters and stuffing put on the dog here! But just see how simple to fix.
Bake at 350° for 40 minutes. Makes 4 servings

2 *large onions, chopped (2 cups)*
4 *tablespoons (½ stick) butter or margarine*
5 *tablespoons thawed frozen concentrate for orange juice (from a 6-ounce can)*
¾ *cup water*

1 *package (8 ounces) ready-mix bread stuffing*
8 *frankfurters, halved crosswise*
1 *tablespoon honey*
16 *small stuffed green olives*

1 Sauté onions in butter or margarine until soft in a medium-size saucepan.
2 Stir in 4 tablespoons of the orange-juice concentrate and water; heat to boiling. Pour over stuffing mix in a large bowl; toss until evenly

moist. Spoon into a lightly greased 5- or 6-cup soufflé dish or straight-side baking dish.

3 Stand frankfurter halves around edge in dish, pushing them about halfway down into stuffing; cover with foil.

4 Bake in moderate oven (350°) 30 minutes; uncover.

5 Mix remaining 1 tablespoon orange-juice concentrate with honey in a cup; brush part over frankfurters.

6 Continue baking, brushing once or twice more with remaining orange mixture, 10 minutes, or until frankfurters are richly glazed.

7 Thread each olive onto a wooden pick; stick into tops of frankfurters just before serving.

●

Upside-Down Frankfurter Bake
Bake at 400° for 25 minutes. Makes 6 servings

1 medium-size onion, chopped (½ cup)
1 green pepper, chopped (½ cup)
1 tablespoon drippings
1 can (about 1 pound) tomatoes
2 tablespoons brown sugar
1 teaspoon dry mustard
1 teaspoon salt
1 crumbled bay leaf
½ teaspoon leaf basil, crumbled
1 package (10 ounces) frozen lima beans
1 package corn-muffin mix
8 frankfurters (about 1 pound)

1 Sauté onion and green pepper in drippings in large frying pan 5 minutes, or just until tender.

2 Stir in tomatoes, brown sugar, mustard, salt, bay leaf and basil; add lima beans; cover; heat to boiling; reduce heat; cook 10 minutes, stirring once to separate beans.

3 While bean mixture cooks, prepare corn-muffin mix according to directions on package for corn bread.

4 Arrange frankfurters in baking pan, 11x7x2; cover with hot bean mixture; carefully spoon corn-bread batter in an even layer over beans.

5 Bake in hot oven (400°) 25 minutes; remove and let cool 5 minutes; loosen around edges; invert onto platter.

●

Carnival Casserole
Bake at 375° for 40 minutes. Makes 6 servings

1 package (12 ounces) frozen rice pilaf in convenience cooking pouch

1 pound frankfurters
1 can (12 ounces) niblet corn, drained
1 can (10½ ounces) condensed cream of celery soup
4 ounces process pasteurized cheese spread (from an 8-ounce package)

1 Place rice pouch in a large bowl; fill with *very* hot water; let stand 5 minutes.

2 Cut 2 of the frankfurters in half lengthwise, then in half crosswise; reserve for topping. Cut remaining frankfurters into ½-inch slices; mix with corn and soup in a medium-size bowl. Cut cheese spread into 4 thin slices; cut each slice diagonally; reserve for topping.

3 Remove rice from pouch; break into small pieces; place in bottom of a 6-cup baking dish; top with frankfurter mixture, spreading evenly.

4 Bake in moderate oven (350°) 20 minutes. Place reserved frankfurters on top in pinwheel design; top each frankfurter with a section of cheese. Bake 20 minutes longer, or until cheese is melted and casserole is bubbly in the center.

Confetti Skillet Supper
An all-in-one dish to serve on one of those busy days just before Christmas.
Makes 6 servings

½ cup uncooked regular rice
1 medium-size onion, chopped (½ cup)
2 tablespoons butter or margarine
1 can (1 pound) stewed tomatoes
1 package (10 ounces) frozen baby lima beans
1 package (10 ounces) frozen whole kernel corn
2 teaspoons salt
¼ teaspoon pepper
1 pound frankfurters

1 Sauté rice and onion in butter or margarine until onion is soft in frying pan; stir in next five ingredients.

2 Score tops of frankfurters; halve each; stir into rice mixture; cover tightly.

3 Simmer 30 minutes, or until liquid is absorbed and rice is tender; fluff up with fork just before serving.

●

Bowwow Burgers
Franks and hamburgers taste twice as good served together, and these have a bonus cheese stuffing.
Bake at 350° for 12 minutes. Makes 8 servings

Here's bright budget fare; Confetti Skillet Supper.

8 frankfurters

1 package (8 ounces) sliced process American cheese
1 pound ground beef
1 teaspoon salt
⅛ teaspoon pepper

1 Slit each frankfurter lengthwise. Cut cheese (no need to separate slices) into 8 even-wide strips; stuff one into each frankfurter.
2 Season ground beef with salt and pepper; divide into 8 even mounds. Place each between two squares of wax paper; press into a large patty about ¼ inch thick. Wrap each patty around the middle of a stuffed frankfurter, using wax paper as a rolling guide. (Ends of frankfurters will be uncovered.) Place meat in a lightly greased large shallow baking pan.
3 Bake in moderate oven (350°) 12 minutes, or until beef is done as you like it and frankfurters are puffy hot. Serve plain or in frankfurter rolls with prepared mustard or bottled catsup if you wish.

Chili Franks
Bake at 425° for 15 minutes. Makes 6 servings

12 frankfurters
½ cup chili sauce
1 packet (2 to an envelope) toasted onion dip mix
½ cup chopped pimiento-stuffed olives

1 Slit each frankfurter lengthwise about three quarters of the way through; open each out flat and place in a single layer in a shallow baking pan.
2 Blend chili sauce, dip mix, and olives in a small bowl. Spoon over center of each frankfurter.
3 Bake in hot oven (425°) 15 minutes, or until sauce is bubbly.

Bohemian Salad
Bake at 350° about 40 minutes. Makes 6 servings

1 can (about 1 pound) sauerkraut
3 cups diced cold cooked potatoes
1 cup finely diced raw carrots
¼ teaspoon caraway seeds
3 strips bacon, diced
1 small onion, chopped (¼ cup)

Simple twist—bacon spiraling grilled frankfurters.

½ cup chopped celery
1 egg
⅓ cup water
⅓ cup sauerkraut juice (from can)
⅓ cup cider vinegar
8 frankfurters (about 1 pound), cut in thirds

1 Drain sauerkraut; save ⅓ cup juice for Step 4; combine sauerkraut with potatoes, carrots and caraway seeds in large bowl.
2 Fry bacon in medium-size frying pan until crisp; drain on absorbent paper; stir into sauerkraut mixture.
3 Sauté onion and celery in bacon fat in pan 5 minutes, or until golden; add to sauerkraut mixture.
4 Beat egg slightly in small bowl; stir in water, sauerkraut juice and vinegar; pour into frying pan; cook over low heat, stirring constantly, until sauce thickens; stir into sauerkraut mixture.
5 Layer frankfurters and sauerkraut mixture in 6-cup baking dish; cover.
6 Bake in moderate oven (350°) about 40 minutes, or until heated through.

Curried Wiener Ring
Bake at 325° for 30 minutes. Makes 4 servings

1 cup uncooked regular rice
3 tablespoons butter or margarine
1 teaspoon curry powder
½ teaspoon dry mustard
1 large onion, chopped (1 cup)
1 tart apple, pared, cored and chopped
1 cup chopped celery
1 small can (⅔ cup) evaporated milk
½ cup water
8 frankfurters (about 1 pound)

1 Cook rice, following label directions on package.
2 While rice cooks, melt butter or margarine in large frying pan; add curry powder, dry mustard, onion, apple and celery; sauté slowly 10 minutes; stir in evaporated milk and water; combine with cooked rice in 8-cup baking dish.
3 Halve frankfurters, then split lengthwise; stir all but 8 pieces into rice mixture; arrange remaining pieces in ring on top; cover.
4 Bake in slow oven (325°) 30 minutes to blend flavors.

Wiener Salad Bake
Bake at 350° for 45 minutes. Makes 6 servings

Beans and franks team up in Halakahiki Bean Bake.

3 tablespoons butter or margarine
3 tablespoons all-purpose flour
1 teaspoon salt
¾ teaspoon dry mustard
¼ teaspoon pepper
1½ cups milk
¾ cup mayonnaise or salad dressing
6 medium-size potatoes, cooked, peeled and diced
1 can (about 1 pound) cut green beans, drained
1 medium-size onion, chopped
6 frankfurters, cut into ¼-inch-thick diagonal slices
2 tablespoons buttered coarse bread crumbs

1 Melt butter or margarine in small saucepan; remove from heat; blend in flour, salt, mustard and pepper; slowly stir in milk.
2 Cook over medium heat, stirring constantly, until mixture thickens and boils 1 minute; remove from heat; blend in mayonnaise or salad

dressing; measure ¼ cup sauce; save for Step 4.

3 Fold potatoes, green beans, onion and three quarters of the frankfurter slices into remaining sauce; spoon into baking dish, 8- to 10-cup size.

4 Arrange remaining frankfurters in a ring on top; spoon reserved ¼ cup sauce over frankfurters; sprinkle with buttered crumbs.

5 Bake in moderate oven (350°) 45 minutes, or until bubbly-hot.

Plank Franks

Bake at 425° about 20 minutes. Makes 4 servings

8 frankfurters (about 1 pound)
3 cups seasoned mashed potatoes
2 slices Muenster or brick cheese, cut in 1-inch squares
2 tomatoes, quartered

1 Split frankfurters almost through and open flat; put each two together, sandwich fashion, with about ½ cup mashed potato between; place on plank or ovenproof platter to form a cross.

2 Fill center with remaining mashed potato; top all with cheese squares.

3 Bake in hot oven (425°) about 20 minutes, or until cheese is golden; garnish with tomato wedges; serve with hot buttered cabbage.

Halakahiki Bean Bake

Glazed frankfurters and pineapple rings make canned baked beans fancy picnic fare.
Bake at 400° about 35 minutes. Makes 4 servings

2 cans (about 1 pound each) beans in tomato sauce
½ small onion, grated
¼ cup molasses
1 tablespoon prepared mustard
4 frankfurters (about ½ pound), cut in half crosswise
1 can (about 9 ounces) sliced pineapple, drained

1 Combine beans and grated onion in medium-size bowl.

2 Mix molasses and mustard in 1-cup measure; stir half into beans (save remaining for Step 4). Spoon beans into 4 individual casseroles or into a 6-cup casserole.

3 Bake, covered, in hot oven (400°) 25 minutes, or until bubbly-hot; remove from oven.

4 Score frankfurter halves about ¼ inch deep;

arrange with pineapple slices on top of beans; brush with half of saved molasses mixture.

5 Return to oven; bake 5 minutes; brush again with molasses mixture; bake 5 minutes longer, or until richly glazed.

Bean Bake Royale

Bake at 400° about 40 minutes. Makes 6 servings

6 tablespoons molasses
3 tablespoons prepared mustard
2 tablespoons cider vinegar
1 teaspoon instant minced onion
3 cans (about 1 pound each) oven-baked beans
1 pound frankfurters, cut in half
1½ cups biscuit mix
½ cup milk
2 tablespoons melted butter or margarine
⅓ cup cornmeal

1 Combine molasses and mustard in measuring cup; spoon out 2 tablespoons for brushing franks; stir vinegar and onion into remainder.

2 Empty beans into an 8-cup shallow baking dish; stir in molasses-onion mixture; arrange cut frankfurters in chevron design down middle; brush with part of molasses mixture.

3 Bake in hot oven (400°) about 20 minutes, or until bubbly-hot.

4 Blend biscuit mix with milk and follow label directions for rolled biscuits; shape into sixteen 2-inch-long rolls; dip in melted butter or margarine; roll in cornmeal; place around edge of hot baking dish.

5 Brush franks with remaining molasses mixture; bake 20 minutes longer, or until biscuits are done.

Busy-Day Macaroni

Bake at 350° for 30 minutes. Makes 6 servings

1 package (8 ounces) elbow macaroni
1 can (10½ ounces) cream of mushroom soup
1 cup milk
1 cup grated process American cheese (half an 8-ounce package)
1 small onion, grated
2 tablespoons chopped parsley
2 teaspoons prepared mustard
2 teaspoons Worcestershire sauce
8 frankfurters (about 1 pound), cut in ¼-inch rings

1 Cook macaroni in a large amount of boiling salted water just until tender; drain well.

2 Mix macaroni, cream of mushroom soup, milk, cheese, onion, parsley, mustard and Worcestershire sauce in 2-quart baking dish; fold in frankfurter slices.
3 Bake in moderate oven (350°) about 30 minutes, or until bubbly-hot and lightly flecked with brown.

Penny-Ring Pizza
Makes one 14-inch pizza

1 package pizza-pie mix
   Half of an 8-ounce package Muenster, brick, or mozzarella cheese, thinly sliced
·4 frankfurters (about ½ pound), cut in thin rings

1 Mix and shape pizza dough into one large round, following directions on package.
2 Spread with sauce from package; top with cheese and frankfurters.
3 Bake, following package directions, until edges are golden and cheese is bubbly-hot.
4 Cut into 6 wedges; serve hot, with grated Parmesan cheese, if you wish.

Chef's Salad Bowl
Evening warm? Turn frankfurters into this just-hearty-enough main-dish treat.
Makes 8 generous servings

8 cups broken mixed salad greens
8 frankfurters, halved lengthwise and cross-wise and cut in strips
1 package (8 ounces) sliced process American cheese, cut in thin strips
1 package (8 ounces) sliced process Swiss cheese, cut in thin strips
1 pint cherry tomatoes, halved
4 hard-cooked eggs, shelled and sliced
¼ cup grated Parmesan cheese
1 cup bottled French dressing

1 Place greens in a large salad bowl. Arrange frankfurters, American and Swiss cheeses, cherry tomatoes and hard-cooked eggs in sections, spoke fashion, on top. Sprinkle with Parmesan cheese.
2 Just before serving, drizzle with dressing; toss to mix well.

Vienna Sausages and Potato Salad
Peppy franks team with potatoes in a mellow sweet-sour dressing.
Makes 6 servings

9 medium-size potatoes (about 3 pounds), pared and diced
1 small onion, chopped (¼ cup)
1 cup thinly sliced celery
½ cup thinly sliced dill pickle
2 cans (about 4 ounces each) Vienna sausages, sliced
2 tablespoons butter or margarine
2 tablespoons brown sugar
2 tablespoons cider vinegar
2 tablespoons water
½ teaspoon dry mustard
¼ teaspoon salt

1 Cook potatoes in boiling salted water just until tender in medium-size saucepan; drain. Stir in onion, celery and pickle.
2 Sauté Vienna sausages lightly in butter or margarine in large frying pan; mix in remaining ingredients; heat just to boiling.
3 Pour over potato mixture in saucepan; toss lightly. Serve hot.

Bavarian Frank Salad
Sliced wieners team with four vegetables and a double-good dressing for this new twist on hot potato salad.
Makes 4 servings

4 medium-size potatoes, pared and sliced ¼ inch thick
4 medium-size carrots, pared and sliced ¼ inch thick
2 cups thinly sliced celery
1 large onion, chopped (1 cup)
8 frankfurters, sliced ¼ inch thick
2 tablespoons butter or margarine
1 tablespoon sugar
½ teaspoon salt
⅛ teaspoon pepper
2 tablespoons cider vinegar
2 tablespoons water
¼ cup mayonnaise or salad dressing
1 tablespoon sweet-pickle relish

1177

1 Cook potatoes with carrots, celery and onion, covered, in boiling salted water in a medium-size saucepan 15 minutes, or until tender; drain. Place in a large bowl.
2 While vegetables cook, sauté frankfurters in butter or margarine until lightly browned in a medium-size frying pan. Stir in sugar, salt, pepper, vinegar and water; heat to boiling; pour over vegetables. Toss lightly to mix. Let stand about 15 minutes to season.
3 Mix mayonnaise or salad dressing and pickle relish in a cup; fold into potato mixture.

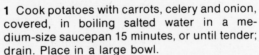

INFALLIBLE INSTANTS

AND MIXES

INFALLIBLE INSTANTS AND MIXES: NEAT TRICKS WITH CONVENIENCE FOODS, SPLIT-SECOND SOUPS, ZIP-QUICK RIB-STICKING MEATS, EASY-TO-FIX FISH AND FOWL, JIG-TIME VEGETABLES SLEIGHT-OF-HAND SALADS, MADE-IN-MINUTES BREADS AND SANDWICHES, MAGIC MIX-BASED DESSERTS.

Hard to think what cooking was like in years past when *everything* had to be made from scratch—soups, stocks, breads, even yeasts and gelatins, not to mention butters and creams. Today, of course, these foods are ready and waiting at the nearest supermarket. In addition, there are literally hundreds of instants, mixes and convenience foods available. And more arriving almost daily.

They're infallible in that they're always close at hand, that they do not only what they promise but also considerably more. A can of consommé or clear broth, for example, makes a particularly savory stock for soup or stew. Refrigerated crescent roll dough can be rolled into flaky pastries, condensed and creamed soups can serve as sauces, slice-and-bake cookies as pie-crusts. Cake mixes can be transformed into quick puddings, pancake mixes into crêpes, biscuit mixes into crusts and cobblers.

The true beauty of convenients—in addition to the hours they save the cook—is their astonishing adaptability. The possibilities are fascinating. And as endless as each cook's ingenuity.

Proof of the magic of mixes: Duchess Vegetables (at left), Frosty Tomato Cream (right), Mantilla Braid (front), a quickie canned meat casserole (behind).

TODAY'S "INSTANTS"

Time, work, money—these are your three big savings with convenience foods. These wonders in a package help you whip up a meal or turn out a fancy dish almost magically. They take the fuss and uncertainty out of cooking and open a whole new world of short cuts to making old favorites. And what morale boosters for beginning cooks! Does all this service cost more? Not if you figure that your time, too, is worth money.

What Are "Convenience Foods"?

They are more than just "mixes." In fact, some of our old-time everyday standbys—evaporated milk, condensed soup, baked beans, deviled ham—are really convenience-food firsts. As newer ones come along, they offer more and more built-in maid service. Paring, chopping, sieving, grating, mixing and even basic measuring are done for you in the food manufacturer's kitchen. At home you have the fun of cooking and the chance to be creative without all of the fussy beforehand work.

What They Can Do for You:

When there's little time to mealtime, choose foods that can be served just as they come from package or can, or those that need heating only.

1179

INFALLIBLE INSTANTS AND MIXES

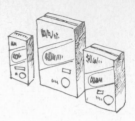

Frozen dinners, or table-ready meats, with frozen or canned seasoned vegetables, packaged rolls, ice cream, bakery-made cake and instant tea or coffee, all help you get a most inviting meal on the table in a jiffy.

When you want to make a special dish, use quick-to-fix convenience foods for most of the meal. Then with the time you've saved, you can fuss a bit with a specialty. If it's a main dish, for example, call on instant potatoes, bottled dressing for the salad, frozen pie for dessert. All are ready fast with hardly a bit of work.

When you want to create a new dish, look to convenience foods, as here's where they rate extra-high. Mixing two or three together saves time—often money—and how good they taste! Here's just one example: Mix a can of frozen cream of shrimp soup with a can of crabmeat, top with grated cheese, and you have a company casserole with precious little fussing. Remember that it's not how long you spend cooking that counts, but how food tastes.

How to Buy Them Wisely:

Convenience foods are really "foods with value added." When you shop for them, think of the convenience "plus" they offer you, since you don't buy all of them for the same reason. Consider these facts:

1. **Convenience of Size**—Regular and large-size tea bags, regular and family-size pudding mixes and fruit-flavor gelatins, handy individual cups or half gallons of ice cream give you a few servings or a lot, as you wish.

2. **Convenience of Preparation**—Soup, sauce and gravy mixes, frozen and canned main dishes and vegetables, packaged cheese dips, frozen piecrusts and cake mixes all cut preparation time.

3. **Convenience of Variety**—The wonderful array of cereals, crackers, bottled salad dressings and seasoning mixes, refrigerated biscuits and sweet rolls, frozen and packaged desserts helps you keep menus interesting and takes the monotony out of cooking.

4. **Convenience of Packaging**—Piecrust in *two sticks,* biscuit mix in *one-cup* packages, *family-size* canned foods, frozen *soup-to-dessert dinners* in a tray are features that influence your buying. Other examples: Instant mashed potatoes packaged with a gravy mix; dessert topping and colorful cake-decorating frosting in pressurized cans.

1180

How They Can Save You Money:

A dish that is quicker or easier to prepare need not cost more, as time—particularly kitchen time—is worth money, too. Proof comes from a United States Department of Agriculture study of 158 convenience foods. Says the report: "If a reasonable value were put on the homemaker's time, many more convenience foods would have a lower cost than fresh or homemade." It is a wise homemaker who learns that housework is one thing there is no catching up with. You go to bed at night thinking everything's done. But as you sleep, sheets are wrinkling, dust is settling and stomachs are getting empty. Thanks go to convenience foods for helping to make the cooking part a lot easier.

PLAN A NO-WORK PICNIC

Yes, a picnic can be a picnic for everybody—even Mom—with the large variety of pack-up-and-go, ready-to-eat foods available to us. So if you're tired of making and wrapping sandwiches, stirring up salads, icing beverages, start your picnic at the supermarket. Here you'll find everything you need, ready in the time it takes to shop—and thrifty enough for many a repeat family eating-outing. Just look at these convenience-food choices:

Main Course

Check over the dozens of varieties of cold cuts, plus canned or cooked sliced ham, for sandwiches or cold plates. Chicken in cans or glass jars makes popular fare, or pick up the freshly barbecued or rotisseried kind for serving hot or cold. Cheese comes in just about every kind, shape and form you could wish for. Please fish fans with canned tuna, salmon, sardines, lobster, shrimps. And if you're ambitious enough to get the fire going, there are the old reliables: Ground beef, frankfurters and small steaks.

Salads

Look in the dairy cabinet or delicatessen section for coleslaw, potato, macaroni, vegetable and fruit-gelatin salads. Buy tomatoes, celery, cucumbers, sweet onions and a host of other fresh items at the produce counter.

Grocery Extras
Mustard, pickles, olives, potato and corn chips, pretzels, crackers, peanut butter, salted nuts, salad dressing and hard-candy mints spark any picnic meal.

Bakery Bonuses
Choose from the wide array of buns, breads and rolls, and for sweet treats—cakes, cup cakes, doughnuts, cookies, pies.

Dessert and Beverage
Pick up fresh melons or grapes, peaches, plums, pears, to eat plain or with cheese. Buy soft drinks, instant coffee or tea, canned fruit juices and milk to serve frosty-cold.

Picnic Supplies
Remember paper plates, cups, napkins, forks and spoons so you'll have nothing to bring back home to wash. The one exception: if you're cooking out, there are charcoal and fire lighter. . . . And some supermarkets even sell ice by the bag.

Home Storage—Most convenience items are packaged in neatly designed containers that protect the high quality of the food, keep it fresh and make storage on the kitchen shelf or in the refrigerator or freezer easy.

Preparation Time—How much time do you have to prepare a dish or a meal? Convenience foods such as meat balls and spaghetti or beef stew offer almost instant service—just open, heat and eat. Or these same foods can serve as a base or a stretcher for another dish. For example, stuff spaghetti into green-pepper halves for baking. Add a refrigerated-biscuit topping and leftover cooked vegetables to canned chicken or beef stew for a deep-dish pie, or stir cut-up cold meat into a canned sauce to serve over rice or noodles. Besides the speed, there is little or no waste, you use fewer utensils and cleanup is almost nil.

Cost—New users may think the cost outweighs the convenience, but even your food budget can get a lift, says the United States Department of Agriculture. In a recent study of 158 convenience foods, 42 were found to be thriftier than their less-convenient counterparts, and the ones most often used are: Frozen and canned orange juice, instant coffee, frozen limas, canned spaghetti, chicken chow mein and devil's food cake mix. Some of the foods that cost more: Ready-to-heat potato products, frozen chicken and turkey dinners, brown 'n' serve yeast rolls, frozen broccoli, precooked rice. But if you are realistic and figure your own preparation time, even these price tags sparkle.

TIPS ON BUYING INSTANTS AND MIXES

To Buy or Not to Buy
Not all convenience foods, instants, and mixes—or whatever you call them—offer the same advantages to each of us. Ask yourself some questions. Will it save you time or work? Is it as good or better than you can make or know how to make? Does your family like it? Will it introduce a new food idea to your table?

To Be a Good-Shopper
Be Selective. Look for those products that will give you the most built-in maid service for the least money. Consider these facts:

Shopping Time—It is quicker and easier to pick up a convenience food than it is to shop for all the ingredients you'll need to make the same dish from scratch. For example, buying a can of vegetable soup takes only a minute; picking out ingredients for a do-it-yourself soup—14 minutes.

NEAT TRICKS WITH CONVENIENCE FOODS

1181

Today more and more wives are returning to work. With their families growing up, they want to turn leisure time into paid time. The rise in sales of convenience foods has paralleled this sharp increase in the number of homemakers employed outside the home, says our Government. Too, new cooks—the fast-growing under-20 brides' market—are learning the uses and advantages of these high-quality wonder foods. Here are a few quick tips for all:

Potato Dress-ups—You name it—frozen puffs, patties, hashed browned, fancy-cut French fries or packaged au gratin, scalloped and mashed varieties—can all be found in the frozen-food cabinets and on the grocery shelves. One romantic note: These products have made potatoes popular again; sales of this dependable fresh standby had been falling for years. Here are a few ways to get the most from these helpers:

Home-Crisp French Fries—Get out your electric skillet or a large frying pan, pour in vegetable oil to a depth of about 1 inch, and add a single layer of frozen French fries. With everything cold to start with, set your electric skillet at 375° or place frying pan over medium heat, and cook, stirring often, just 15 to 20 minutes to make the crispiest brown beauties imaginable.

Golden Patties—Brush frozen potato squares with butter or margarine, sprinkle with salt and pepper, and bake along with ham steak, meat loaf or Swiss steak until crisp and golden. Or, for hashed-in-cream potatoes, break up the frozen patties in a buttered frying pan, and as they heat, stir in evaporated milk. Another tip: Sprinkle with grated cheese for potatoes au gratin, skillet style.

Casserole Magic—Start with precooked rice or macaroni, or curried, Spanish or Chinese fried-rice mix (they're ready-seasoned), add a can of flaked drained tuna or diced canned luncheon meat or cut-up meat from a Sunday roast. If you need a sauce or gravy, choose canned tomato or spaghetti sauce or one of the fancy sauce mixes—sour cream, cheese or onion—and heat all together on top of the range or in the oven to mellow flavors.

Vegetable Easies—Look in the frozen-food cabinet for plain and mixed vegetables, each with its own seasoning mix. Some are packed in transparent envelopes to drop into a pan of boiling water and heat, following label directions. Others have the seasoning mixed in, making a tasty sauce as the vegetable cooks. Serve them separately or combine two such as broccoli and cauliflower, green beans and wax beans, mushrooms and peas with onions.

1182

Dessert Bonuses—What's for dessert is always a problem when you can't plan ahead for the sweet-tooth members of your family. Packaged pudding mix that doubles as pie filling as well as a creamy treat in a cup comes in so many flavors—butterscotch, banana-cream, chocolate, to name just a few. Or stir butterscotch- or semisweet-chocolate-flavor pieces into vanilla or chocolate pudding . . . heat cherry-pie filling to spoon over freshly baked cake squares made from a mix . . . make a double-orange dessert with reconstituted frozen orange juice and orange-flavor gelatin . . . and remember store-bought fresh and frozen pastries, for the convenience of ready-to-eat sweets can turn many a skimpy meal into a feast.

READY-TO-GO SEASONERS

The marvelous world of instants grows and grows—better and better! And hardly a day passes without another new blend in can or package arriving to give cooking a boost.

Dip Mixes—With an envelope of these modern marvels, plus water, milk, sour cream, cream cheese or cottage cheese, you're off in a jiffy to an expertly blended appetizer treat to go with crackers and chips. Most varieties combine nonfat dry milk or dehydrated sour cream with shortening, herbs and spices. Among your flavor choices: Green or toasted onion, garlic, spicy cheese or blue cheese, horseradish, Caesar or barbecue. In addition to their use for dip-making, these dependables can season a cheese filling for celery or a sandwich, a sauce for vegetables or a buttery spread for steak or hamburgers. In supermarkets that stock foreign foods, you may come across canned Mexican cheese dip or *jalapeño* bean dip—a blend of pinto beans, *jalapeño* peppers and seasonings.

Gravy Mixes—Take your pick of dry mixes, liquid or paste gravy bases or canned ready-to-use gravies. Look for dry mixes in foil envelopes or 5-ounce jars to combine with water, milk or meat drippings. Among the popular flavors are beef, chicken, onion, herb, mushroom and brown gravies. Gravy bases in beef or chicken flavors or gravy browning sauce may be stirred into cream or water gravy for extra heartiness, richness or color. Quickest of all to get on the table are the heat-and-eat gravies. Choose beef, chicken or mushroom to suit your fancy. Besides being a favorite with mashed potatoes, canned gravies prove their versatility in stews or casseroles, as a stretcher for homemade gravy or as a topper for hot meat sandwiches.

Salad-Dressing Mixes—Primarily these instants in handy envelopes combine dry herbs and spices. When blended with vegetable or olive oil, vinegar and water, each packet makes about a cup of dressing to toss with your favorite green salad. Name your flavor and you can probably get it: Italian, garlic or garlic-French, Caesar, onion, Parmesan, blue cheese, bacon, cheese-garlic, creamy or regular French, Russian. No time at all? Call on bottled dressings with the mixing done for you.

Sauce Mixes—In both dry mixes and canned ready-to-use products you'll find varieties to suit just about every cooking need. Most dry mixes call for water, milk, sour cream, tomato paste or sauce. Some take cooking and others do not, so follow the label how-tos in fixing. Probably the leader of all is spaghetti-sauce mix, with or without tomato. To dress up other everyday dishes, call upon these sauce-mix specialties:

White, cheese, curry, onion, hollandaise, sour cream, barbecue, taco, Stroganoff, tartar and Spanish rice. More heat-and-they're-ready sauces: Pizza, marinara, Newburg, onion-mushroom, enchilada. To enhance rice, ravioli, pizza, spaghetti, macaroni or Italian-style meat dishes, the tomato instants are excellent. Others go perfectly with vegetables, casseroles, left-over meats, eggs, fish or noodles.

Meat Seasoners and Marinades—All come in handy packets, boxes or jars and blend spices,

1183

Want an instant Hollandaise? Take 1 cup mayonnaise, smooth in 2 tablespoons of melted butter and the strained juice of half a freshly squeezed lemon.

herbs and other ingredients to give meats a distinctive flavor or extra tenderness. The dry seasoners can be mixed into ground beef for hamburgers, meat loaf or slumgullion, or combined with beef for stewing before cooking. In using instant meat marinade, mix it with liquid, pour over meat and let stand at least 15 minutes before cooking.

Soups—Not to be overlooked in any story on seasoners is the soup family; here is the matriarch of all instants and probably the most versatile. All rate tops as soup, of course, but they also take high honors for saucing vegetables, meats, pasta, casseroles or fish; for using as a cooking liquid for meats or as a base for gravy, chowder, rabbit or fricassee. Leaders in popularity are canned condensed soups, which number about three dozen varieties. In contrast to these standbys, there are the specialty products that carry a higher price tag but are ready to use just as they come from the can: Gazpacho, Senegalese, vichyssoise, petite marmite, crab bisque, cream of lobster or shrimp, black bean with sherry and borsch.

Among your choices in frozen condensed soups are clam chowder, oyster stew, cream of potato or shrimp, green pea and vegetable. In packaged dry soup mixes you can pick chicken or chicken-noodle, vegetable, beef-noodle, tomato-vegetable, potato, onion, green pea, chicken-rice and cream of mushroom. You simply add water and cook. And long taken for granted are the old reliables: Canned broth, bouillon and consommé; instant broth in tiny envelopes; bouillon cubes; and liquid or paste beef or chicken extracts or concentrates.

When You Shop:
With seasoning mixes, it's important to check the label on every product you buy, for some can be used right from the package or can to boost flavor or to replace seasoning ingredients in a recipe, while others need to be mixed with liquid first. Usually these factors account for the difference in brands and in prices.

Should you stock up on these items? It's rarely necessary, for prices hold fairly steady, although you may get a break on an introductory offer. More important to consider is that variety in your cupboard can often save your dinner in an emergency.

In shopping you may have to look for these products, for they're often located all around

the store. Good spots to check: Spice-and-herb, salad-dressing, meat, canned-meat, vegetable, and snack departments. If you don't find what you want, ask your supermarket manager.

What about Price?
A sauce that is easier or quicker to prepare from a mix need not cost more than the made-from-scratch variety. In fact, it is often thriftier, if you count *your* time, the product's all-purpose use, the cost of the ingredients that go into it, plus the storage space all of the separate items would take.

To show you how to figure costs for yourself, here are two examples: (1) If you were fixing vegetable soup from scratch, you'd need stock or broth, several vegetables, and two or three herbs or spices. Jot down the cost of each of these items, add them, and then compare the total with the price of dry vegetable-soup mix making the same quantity. Or (2) figure the cost of all of the ingredients that go into your favorite recipe for spaghetti sauce. Then compare this total with the cost of an all-in-one packaged mix or a can of the ready-to-heat variety.

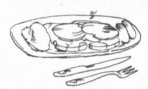

"SOME MAGIC WITH SEASONING MIXES"

- Beat an 8-ounce package of cream cheese until fluffy; stir in 1 can thawed frozen condensed cream of shrimp soup with a few tablespoons milk and lemon juice to taste. Serve as a dip.
- Cook stewing chicken in water seasoned with several chicken-bouillon cubes for double-good broth.
- Simmer tiny whole potatoes or onions in canned chicken broth, then thicken the liquid to serve as gravy.
- Vary the flavor of Swiss steak by adding dry spaghetti-sauce mix, canned spaghetti sauce or hamburger seasoning mix to the liquid called for in your favorite recipe. Or try chili seasoning mix with pot roast.
- Stir a bit of liquid or paste beef extract into packaged white sauce mix for a quick gravy.
- Heat 1 can condensed cream of chicken soup with ¼ cup mayonnaise or salad dressing and 1 tablespoon lemon juice until bubbly; spoon over freshly cooked broccoli or asparagus.
- Prepare Italian salad-dressing mix, following label directions; brush over chicken before broiling or grilling outdoors.

From a box, a high and hand-some cake, frosted with "canned frosting," trimmed with fresh apples.

THE BAKE-DAY MAGIC OF "MIXES"

Most mixes need only a simple shaping trick or a few of your own ingredients to create a homemade-tasting specialty. Notes here will remind you of a few of the many dependables that are available in your supermarket.

Cake Mixes—What a treasure trove of ideas these thrifties offer, and adapting them into your own showy fancies takes little more than imagination. For example: Bake them as layers, loaves, rings, cupcakes, upside-down cakes, petits fours or cookies; stir nuts, fruits, spices or food colorings into the batter; vary the flavor; or finish off with an unusual frosting or filling. Believe it or not, with these few simple tricks, you could make a different cake treat every day for weeks without ever repeating.

Tops in flavor popularity are the standards—white, yellow, chocolate, spice and angel cakes—but most supermarkets go all out to bring you up to a dozen or more other flavors. Among them you'll find lemon, banana, orange,

Baker's secret recipes? Hardly. Everything here actually comes from a mix—cake, roll or cookie.

pineapple, coconut, marble, caramel and fudge, as well as gingerbread, chiffon and pound cake. To be sure of what you're buying, check the label carefully.

To suit small and large families, cake mixes are available in one- and two-layer sizes. And for super convenience, look for the complete cake-in-a-box that even includes the right-size baking pan.

Frosting Mixes—These partners to cake mixes include four basic types: Seven-minute, or fluffy; whipped; butter, or creamy; and ready-to-spread. Seven-minute types need no cooking—you just add boiling water and beat. To the whipped varieties—every bit as easy to fix—you simply add ice water, then keep the cake chilled, once it's frosted. Butter types call for water plus butter or margarine; and, of course, the ready-to-spread kinds are exactly what their name suggests. All packages as well as the canned ready-to-spread varieties fill and frost an average two-layer cake or a dozen cupcakes. Flavor choices seem almost endless and some even match specific cakes.

Piecrust Mixes—With these handy helpers, pastry-making couldn't be easier. The bread sections of some supermarkets carry baked crusts, and many frozen-food cabinets offer unbaked shells, ready to go into the oven. If you prefer crumb crusts, look for them in foil

1186

pans, in family and individual tart-shell sizes. Since they keep perfectly on the cupboard shelf and need no baking, they're a great dessert-saver on extra-busy days or for company emergencies.

Pie Fillings—Heading this hit parade are canned fruit fillings: Apple, blueberry, pineapple, cherry, mincemeat and peach; plus canned cream types such as chocolate, vanilla, lemon and pumpkin; canned presliced apples to sweeten and spice to your own taste; and a paradise of packaged pie fillings in instant (beat and pour) and ready-to-cook forms. Name your flavor and you can probably get it. Still others that rate top consideration are packaged egg-custard mix and chiffonlike filling mixes that take only whipping and chilling.

Cookie Mixes—If you feel you haven't time for cookie-baking, here's a jiffy way to make dozens of fancies for family or friends. Look for brownie mixes (plain or with nuts), date-bar mix or plain or chocolate-studded cookie mixes. And remember, too, that gingerbread mix can be turned into drop cookies or rolled cutouts, or happy little gingerbread men to charm the children.

Yeast Bread and Roll Mixes—With these modern-day instants, yeast-baking inspiration comes easy. All are packaged with the yeast,

Feathery frozen pattie shells are the foundation of this dessert. Pudding mix provides the filling.

and simple directions tell you how to fix the spongy dough. Call on them as your helpers for making loaves of bread, dinner or sweet rolls, coffee cakes or pizza crusts.

Muffin Mixes—Depend on these quickies to dress up any lunch or dinner or to start your morning off bright. Leading kinds include bran, corn, blueberry, oatmeal, banana-nut, orange and date. Most packages make from six to a dozen tender gems, or, with a little sleight-of-hand, star as coffee cake or loaf bread. Follow the label for directions.

Biscuit Mixes—These old-timers rank high in versatility, and in mere minutes can be made into biscuits, coffee cakes, waffles, cobblers or meat-pie toppers. Most are now packaged in sizes from 6 ounces to 2½ pounds, and especially convenient is a 2-pound box of eight individual packets, each premeasured to hold just one cup of mix.

Quick Breads—Most popular is corn-bread mix in bag or box to bake as a loaf or muffins. For breakfast or coffeetime treats, choose butter-pecan, blueberry, cinnamon-streusel and apple-cinnamon coffeecake mixes, or apricot-nut, date, banana, nut or raisin-spice quick-bread mixes.

YOUR "FINDS" IN THE DAIRY CASE

1188

Biscuits and Dinner Rolls—Flip open a package, and minutes later you have a plateful of golden beauties to make any meal seem downright lavish. To suit your taste, you can pick plain, buttermilk, flaky or country-style biscuits, or Parker House, crescent or swirl-shape rolls. Remember that all refrigerated items are perishable and must be kept chilled until baking time. Each package has a date stamped on it, and to enjoy these products at their best, be sure to use them within the time limit.

Sweet Rolls—What inviting standbys for drop-in guests, coffeetimes or family breakfasts! Each package makes eight rolls and comes with its own icing.

Cookies—Have you young cooks at your house? Buy several rolls of the ready-to-slice-and-bake treats, plus an assortment of frostings in pressurized cans or plastic tubes, colored decorating sugars and tiny candies, and let them have the thrill of making and decorating their very own holiday fancies. Just a few of your flavor choices are butterscotch-nut, fudge-nut, oatmeal-raisin, peanut butter, ginger and sugar. All come in transparent-wrapped sausagelike rolls and make from three to six dozen cookies.

SOME SPLIT-SECOND SOUPS

Frosty Tomato Cream
Makes 6 servings

1 can (10½ ounces) condensed chicken broth, well chilled
1 can (10¾ ounces) condensed tomato soup, well chilled
1 cup light cream or table cream
1 small cucumber, pared and cut up
1 small onion, peeled and cut up
8 sprigs of parsley
Thin cucumber slices
Fresh dill sprigs

1 Skim any fat from chicken broth; combine soups in an electric-blender container. Add light cream or table cream; the cut-up cucumber, the onion and parsley. Cover and beat until almost smooth.
2 Chill several hours or until frosty-cold. Pour into a tureen or small cups or bowls; float thin cucumber slices and fresh dill sprigs on top.

Finnish Fruit "Soup"
Makes 8 servings

1 package (3 ounces) lemon-flavor gelatin

For a zip-quick green pea soup, cook a package of frozen green peas, purée, then thin to a good "soup" consistency with cream.

Finnish Fruit "Soup" is a jiffy combo of canned fruit cocktail and dairy-case citrus fruit salad suspended in lemon gelatin.

1 cup boiling water
1 cup cold water
1 can (1 pound, 13 ounces) fruit cocktail
1 jar (16 ounces) citrus fruit salad (from dairy case)
¼ cup lemon juice

1 Dissolve gelatin in boiling water in a large bowl; stir in cold water, fruit cocktail and syrup, fruit salad and juice and lemon juice. Chill several hours, or until very cold.
2 When ready to serve, ladle into a glass serving bowl or individual serving dishes. Garnish with mint, if you wish. Serve as an appetizer.

Note—If soup chills overnight, gelatin will set softly.

1189

Mushroom Bisque
Makes 4 to 6 servings

1 envelope or 1 can (2 to a package) mushroom soup mix
1 tablespoon grated onion
2 cups water
Dash of ground allspice
1½ cups light cream or table cream
1 teaspoon lemon juice

1 Prepare soup mix with onion and water, following label directions; cool.
2 Beat in remaining ingredients. Chill.
3 Pour into chilled cups or mugs. Garnish with chopped parsley, if you wish.

Clam Stew
Makes 6 servings

1 small onion, minced (¼ cup)
¼ cup minced celery
2 tablespoons butter or margarine
1 can (about 8 ounces) minced clams
3 cups milk
1 teaspoon Worcestershire sauce
   Few drops liquid red pepper seasoning
½ cup dry instant mashed potatoes
1 tablespoon chopped parsley

1 Sauté onion and celery in butter or margarine until soft in a large saucepan.
2 Stir in clams and liquid, milk, Worcestershire sauce and liquid red pepper seasoning. Heat just to boiling; remove from heat.
3 Stir in instant potatoes and parsley until mixture thickens slightly.
4 Ladle into soup bowls or cups. Serve with your favorite crackers.

Pea Soup Chowder
Canned soup, plus chick peas and seasonings, makes this hearty lunch soup.
Makes 4 to 6 servings

1 cup sliced celery
1½ cups water
1 can (11¼ ounces) condensed green-pea soup
1 can (about 1 pound) chick peas
¼ cup chili sauce
1 tablespoon grated onion
¼ teaspoon mixed Italian herbs
1 beef-bouillon cube

1 Simmer celery in water 10 minutes, or just until crisply tender, in a medium-size saucepan.
2 Stir in remaining ingredients, crushing bouillon cube with spoon. Heat to boiling, then simmer 5 minutes.
3 Ladle into heated soup bowls or cups.

Country Chicken Chowder
Canned soup, canned corn, canned milk—what could be easier?
Makes 6 servings

1 medium-size onion, chopped (½ cup)
2 tablespoons butter or margarine
2 cans (10½ ounces each) condensed chicken-noodle soup
1 soup can water
1 can (about 1 pound) cream-style corn
1 small can evaporated milk (⅔ cup)
¼ teaspoon pepper
2 tablespoons chopped parsley

1 Sauté onion in butter or margarine just until soft in medium-size saucepan.
2 Stir in remaining ingredients, except parsley. Heat just to boiling.
3 Pour into heated soup bowls or mugs; sprinkle with parsley.

Confetti Chowder
Makes 8 servings

1 package (12 ounces) smoked sausage links
2 tablespoons butter or margarine
1 large onion, chopped (1 cup)
2 packages (10 ounces each) frozen mixed vegetables
1 cup water
6 cups reconstituted instant nonfat dry milk
1 tablespoon prepared mustard
2 teaspoons salt
¼ teaspoon pepper
1 cup dry instant mashed potatoes

1 Slice sausages 1 inch thick; brown in butter or margarine in a heavy kettle; remove and set aside. Stir onion into drippings; sauté until soft.
2 Stir in mixed vegetables and water; cook, following label directions. Stir in milk, mustard, salt, pepper and sausages. Heat slowly, stirring several times, to boiling.
3 Slowly stir in dry potatoes until mixture thickens slightly. Ladle into heated soup bowls; serve with chowder crackers.

RIB-STICKING MEATS AND MAIN DISHES

Beefeater's Platter
Makes 6 to 8 servings

1 arm-bone beef chuck roast, weighing about
   4 pounds
3 medium-size onions, peeled and sliced thin
1 can (15½ ounces) sandwich sauce
1 cup water
1 package (8 ounces) regular noodles
¼ cup chopped parsley

1 Trim fat from roast. Sauté enough of the trimmings in a heavy kettle or Dutch oven to make about 2 tablespoonfuls drippings; remove and discard.
2 Brown roast slowly in drippings; drain off fat. Stir in onions, sandwich sauce and water. Heat to boiling; cover. Simmer, turning meat several times, 2½ hours, or until tender. Place on a deep serving platter; keep warm.
3 While roast simmers, cook noodles, following label directions; drain. Spoon around roast on platter; sprinkle parsley over noodles.
4 Skim any fat from sauce; reheat to boiling. Spoon part over roast; serve remainder separately. Carve roast into serving-size slices.

Steak Piquant
Man-size chunks of beef bake with noodles, limas and tomatoes in this colorful entrée.
Bake at 350° for 30 minutes. Makes 6 servings

2 pounds lean round steak or beef chuck, cut
   into 1-inch cubes
2 tablespoons vegetable oil
½ cup water
2 beef-bouillon cubes
1½ teaspoons salt
½ teaspoon ground cardamom
¼ teaspoon pepper
1 tablespoon lemon juice
1 package (8 ounces) noodles
1 package (10 ounces) frozen baby lima
   beans
3 medium-size tomatoes, cut into wedges
1 teaspoon sugar
1 tablespoon finely chopped parsley

1 Brown beef cubes in vegetable oil in large frying pan. Stir in water, bouillon cubes, salt, cardamom, pepper and lemon juice. Cover; simmer 20 to 30 minutes, or until meat is tender.
2 Cook noodles, following label directions; drain; place in greased 12-cup baking dish.

3 Cook lima beans, following label directions; drain; spoon over noodles to make a ring around edge of baking dish.
4 Spoon meat in middle, then pour juices over all. Arrange tomato wedges, overlapping, on top of lima beans; sprinkle with sugar and salt and pepper, if desired; cover.
5 Bake in moderate oven (350°) 30 minutes to blend flavors. Sprinkle parsley over top just before serving.

Cubed-Beef Stroganoff
This gourmet dish can be ready in minutes with leftover roast beef.
Makes 6 servings

1 medium-size onion, chopped (½ cup)
2 tablespoons vegetable oil
3 cups cubed cooked beef
1 can (10¾ ounces) condensed tomato soup
1 can (3 or 4 ounces) chopped mushrooms
1 teaspoon sugar
1 cup dairy sour cream

1 Sauté onion in vegetable oil in large frying pan; add beef and brown lightly.
2 Stir in tomato soup, mushrooms and liquid and sugar; cover; simmer 20 minutes to blend flavors.
3 Stir in sour cream; heat just to boiling (don't let sauce boil, as sour cream may curdle). Serve over buttered hot noodles.

Red-Flannel Hash
Makes 4 generous servings

1 can (1 pound) julienne beets
2 cans (1 pound each) corned-beef hash
1 tablespoon instant minced onion

1 Drain beets, then pat dry between sheets of paper toweling.
2 Break up corned-beef hash with a fork in a large bowl; mix in beets and onion. Shape into 8 thick patties.
3 Sauté slowly, turning only once, until crusty-brown in a large frying pan. (No need to add any fat.) Serve hot with catsup or prepared mustard, if you wish.

Four instants (l. to r.): Onion-Sausage Pie, Spinach Salad Imperial, Lemon-Walnut Bread, Beefeater's Platter.

'70s Pizza
Bake at 375° for 20 minutes. Makes 4 servings

1 pound meat loaf mixture
1 tablespoon vegetable oil
1 envelope (1½ ounces) spaghetti sauce mix
1 can (8 ounces) tomato sauce
1 cup water
1 package (8 ounces) refrigerated butterflake dinner rolls
1 cup ricotta cheese
4 ounces mozzarella cheese, shredded (1 cup)
1 tablespoon grated Parmesan cheese

1 Brown meat loaf mixture in oil in a medium-size skillet until no pink remains (about 10 minutes); break into small pieces with a fork; sprinkle with spaghetti sauce mix; stir in tomato sauce, then water. Bring to boiling; reduce heat;

simmer, stirring often, 20 minutes, or until very thick.

2 Remove dinner rolls from package (12 rolls in package); separate each roll to make 24 thinner rolls; place 12 in a layer on bottom of a 9-inch pie plate; press edges together to cover bottom; spoon ½ cup ricotta evenly over roll layer; top with half the cooked meat mixture; sprinkle with ½ cup mozzarella; repeat layers of ricotta, meat and mozzarella; top with remaining rolls.

3 Bake in moderate oven (375°) 15 minutes; sprinkle with Parmesan cheese; bake 5 minutes longer, or until rolls are golden brown. Cut into wedges to serve.

Hungarian Veal

Mild-flavor veal and autumn vegetables bubble temptingly in a creamy-rich gravy.
Bake at 350° for 25 minutes. Makes 6 servings

1½ pounds lean veal shoulder, cut in cubes
¼ cup sifted all-purpose flour

INFALLIBLE INSTANTS AND MIXES

2 teaspoons salt
⅛ teaspoon pepper
2 tablespoons vegetable oil
1½ cups water
12 small white onions, peeled
1 small eggplant, pared and diced
1 cup dairy sour cream
1 teaspoon paprika
2 cans (2¼ ounces each) shoestring potatoes

1 Shake veal with flour, 1 teaspoon salt and pepper in paper bag to coat well. (Save remaining teaspoon of salt for Step 2.)
2 Brown quickly in vegetable oil in large frying pan; stir in water and remaining teaspoon of salt, then add onions and eggplant. Cover; simmer 30 minutes, or until onions are tender.
3 Stir in sour cream and paprika; spoon mixture into an 8-cup baking dish; sprinkle the potatoes evenly over the top.

4 Bake in moderate oven (350°) 25 minutes, or until meat is tender.

Viennese Veal
Makes 6 servings

1½ pounds cubed veal steaks
2 tablespoons vegetable oil
1 can (about 10 ounces) mushroom gravy
½ cup water
1 cup dairy sour cream
¼ cup chopped parsley

1 Cut veal into serving-size pieces; sauté in vegetable oil in large frying pan over medium heat 5 minutes on each side, or until tender; remove veal to a heated platter; keep hot while you make the gravy.
2 Pour all excess fat from pan; stir in mushroom

As dazzlingly red and gold as autumn itself: Harvest Skillet Pork Chops seasoned with frozen fruit juice.

gravy and water; heat to boiling, stirring constantly; simmer 2 to 3 minutes.

3 Remove from heat; stir in sour cream and parsley until well blended; pour around meat; serve at once, as sour cream may curdle if reheated.

Lamb-and-Barley Bake
Bake at 400° for 45 minutes. Makes 8 servings

    1 cup medium barley
    1 envelope (2 to a package) beef flavor
      mushroom mix
    5 cups water
    2 pounds ground-lamb patties
    2 eggs, beaten
    2 tablespoons all-purpose flour
    1 teaspoon salt
    1 teaspoon mixed salad herbs
    2 tablespoons butter or margarine
    1 large onion, chopped (1 cup)
    1 can (1 pound) stewed tomatoes
    ¼ cup chopped parsley

1 Combine barley, mushroom mix and water in a large saucepan; heat to boiling; cover. Simmer, stirring several times, 30 minutes, or until barley is tender and almost all liquid is absorbed. Spoon into a 12-cup baking dish.
2 Break up lamb patties and combine with eggs, flour, salt and salad herbs in a large bowl; mix lightly until well blended. Shape into 24 small balls.
3 Brown in butter or margarine in a large frying pan; remove with a slotted spoon and place in baking dish. Pour all drippings from pan, then measure 2 tablespoonfuls and return to pan.
4 Stir in onion; sauté until soft. Stir in tomatoes; heat to boiling. Pour over meat mixture; stir lightly to mix. Do not cover.
5 Bake in hot oven (400°) 45 minutes, or until bubbly. Sprinkle with parsley.

Chinese Chops
Bake at 350° for 1 hour. Makes 6 servings

    6 loin or rib pork chops, cut ½ inch thick
    ½ teaspoon salt
    1 cup uncooked regular rice
    2½ cups boiling water
    1 tablespoon butter or margarine
    ½ small green pepper, halved, seeded and cut
      in thin strips
    1 can (about 9 ounces) pineapple tidbits
    1 envelope (2 ounces) sweet-sour sauce mix

1 Trim all fat from chops. Sauté a few of the trimmings in a large frying pan; remove and discard. Place chops in drippings; sauté slowly, turning once, until brown; sprinkle with salt.
2 Place rice in a shallow 10-cup baking dish; stir in boiling water and butter or margarine. Place chops in a single layer on top; cover.
3 Bake in moderate oven (350°) 50 minutes; uncover.
4 While chops bake, sauté green pepper until soft in remaining drippings in frying pan.
5 Drain syrup from pineapple into a 2-cup measure; add water to make 1¼ cups. Sprinkle sauce mix over green pepper in pan; stir in pineapple liquid. Heat, stirring constantly, to boiling. Stir in pineapple; simmer, stirring constantly, 1 minute. Pour over chops.
6 Bake 10 minutes longer to blend the flavors.

Harvest Skillet Pork Chops
Makes 6 servings

    1 can (6 ounces) frozen concentrated pineap-
      ple-orange juice
    3 tablespoons soy sauce
    2 teaspoons ground ginger
    ½ teaspoon salt
    ½ teaspoon leaf marjoram, crumbled
    6 loin, rib, or shoulder pork chops, cut ½ inch
      thick
    2 acorn squashes
    3 pickled sweet red peppers, halved

1 Combine unthawed fruit juice, soy sauce, ginger, salt and marjoram in 2-cup measure; let stand while browning chops.
2 Trim excess fat from chops; brown chops well in an electric frying pan or a large heavy frying pan rubbed with fat trimmings; drain all fat from pan; pour fruit-juice mixture over chops.
3 Wash and slice squashes into 1-inch-thick rings; remove seeds; halve each ring; arrange with chops in pan; cover tightly.
4 Simmer, brushing squashes with glaze once or twice, 45 minutes, or until chops are tender. (If using an electric frying pan, set control at 325°.)
5 Put pickled red peppers into pan 5 minutes before chops are done to heat through.

Pork-Potato Scallop
Bake at 400° for 40 minutes. Makes 6 servings

    1 can (12 ounces) pork luncheon meat
    1 can (10½ ounces) condensed cream of as-
      paragus soup
    ½ cup milk

1195

1 small onion, peeled and chopped
¼ teaspoon pepper
4 cups frozen hashed brown potatoes

1 Cut meat into 6 slices; halve slices diagonally. Set aside a few triangles for garnish; arrange remainder in bottom of a 6-cup baking dish.
2 Blend soup, milk, onion and pepper in a medium-size saucepan; heat to boiling; remove from heat. Stir in potatoes; spoon into dish. Top with remaining meat; cover.
3 Bake in hot oven (400°) 40 minutes, or until bubbly-hot.

Dinner Ham Casserole
Meat, vegetables and gravy cook in one dish. Make ahead to bake at mealtime.
Bake at 350° for 30 minutes. Makes 4 servings

1 package (10 ounces) frozen baby lima beans
2 medium-size carrots, scraped and sliced thin (about 1 cup)
1 medium-size cucumber, pared, quartered lengthwise and cubed
3 cups diced cooked lean ham (about 1 pound)
1 medium-size onion, chopped (½ cup)
2 tablespoons butter or margarine
1 can (10½ ounces) condensed cream of celery soup
⅔ cup milk
⅛ teaspoon pepper
1 package (4 ounces) corn chips, crushed

1 Cook lima beans and carrots together, following label directions for limas; add cucumber for last 2 minutes' cooking; drain.
2 Sauté ham and onion in butter or margarine in large frying pan 5 minutes, or until onion is softened. Stir in soup, milk and pepper; heat, stirring constantly, just until blended.
3 Pour into a buttered 6-cup casserole; stir in cooked vegetables; sprinkle crushed corn chips over.
4 Bake in moderate oven (350°) 30 minutes, or until bubbly-hot.
Note—If made in the morning and chilled, take casserole from refrigerator and let stand at room temperature for 30 minutes before putting into oven to bake.

Twin Pork Pizzas
Bake at 400° for 30 minutes. Makes two 14-inch pizzas

2 cans (1 pound each) pork and beans
1 can (8 ounces) tomato sauce with onions
1 teaspoon Italian seasoning
1 teaspoon sugar
2 tablespoons hotdog relish
½ pound sliced bacon, cut in 1-inch pieces
1 package hot-roll mix
   Water
2 tablespoons vegetable oil
½ pound frankfurters, sliced thin
2 packages (4 ounces each) shredded mozzarella cheese

1 Combine beans, tomato sauce, Italian seasoning and sugar in a heavy large saucepan. Heat to boiling, then simmer, stirring several times, 25 minutes, or until mixture is very thick. Remove from heat; stir in relish.
2 Sauté bacon until partly crisp in a medium-size frying pan; remove and drain on paper toweling.
3 Prepare hot-roll mix with water, following label directions for pizza dough. Divide in half; pat each half into an ungreased 14-inch pizza pan. Brush with vegetable oil.
4 Spread bean mixture evenly into shells; top one with bacon pieces and the other with frankfurter slices.
5 Bake in hot oven (400°) 15 minutes; sprinkle cheese over each. Bake 15 minutes longer, or until crust is golden and sauce is bubbly. Cut each in 6 to 8 wedges.

Onion-Sausage Pie
Bake at 375° for 40 minutes. Makes 6 servings

2 frozen ready-to-bake 9-inch piecrusts
1 can (12 or 16 ounces) whole-kernel corn
1 can (about 1 pound) boiled onions with cream-sauce mix
1 can (1 pound) white potatoes, drained and diced
1 package (8 ounces) heat-and-serve sausages, sliced
2 tablespoons butter or margarine
½ teaspoon salt
⅛ teaspoon pepper
2 teaspoons parsley flakes
3 hard-cooked eggs, shelled and diced
1 egg, beaten

1 Thaw both piecrusts, following label directions.
2 Drain liquid from corn into a 1-cup measure; drain liquid from onions; add enough onion liquid to corn liquid to make ¾ cup.
3 Sauté potatoes and sausages in butter or margarine until lightly browned in a large frying

Take a ready-to-heat pizza, add slices of salami, some link sausages and pepperoni and presto! Sausage Pizza.

pan; stir in salt and pepper. Spoon mixture into a large bowl.

4 Stir the ¾ cup liquid into drippings in frying pan; add sauce mix from onions. Cook, stirring constantly, until sauce thickens and boils 1 minute. Stir into meat mixture with corn, onions, parsley flakes and hard-cooked eggs. Spoon into a shallow 6-cup baking dish.

5 Roll out 1 of the piecrusts on a pastry cloth or board to a rectangle, 12x10; working lengthwise, cut into 6 strips ¾ inch wide and 6 strips ¼ inch wide with a pastry wheel or knife. Brush wide strips lightly with part of the beaten egg; press a narrow strip on top of each. Weave strips over filling in dish to make a crisscross top; trim any overhang flush with rim of dish.

6 Repeat rolling, cutting, brushing and stacking with remaining piecrust. Brush ends of strips over filling with beaten egg; place remaining strips around rim of dish, overlapping slightly, to make a neat edge.

7 Bake in moderate oven (375°) 15 minutes; brush strips with remaining beaten egg. Bake 25 minutes longer, or until pastry is golden and filling bubbles up. Garnish with parsley, if you wish.

Note—Cut piecrust trimmings into 2-inch lengths; place on a cookie sheet; sprinkle with salt. Bake in hot oven (425°) 8 minutes, or until golden. Serve with soup or salad or as snacks.

Sausage Pizza
Top heat-and-serve pizza with extra meats and cheese—and pop into the oven.
Makes 6 servings

1 (12-inch) ready-to-heat pizza
6 slices provolone cheese (from an 8-ounce package)
6 slices salami (from an 8-ounce package)
6 smoked link sausages (from a 10- or 12-ounce package)
1 pepperoni (from a 5-ounce package)
Parsley
2 cups cherry tomatoes

1 Place pizza on ungreased pizza pan or large cookie sheet. Cut cheese slices into quarters; cut salami and sausages in half; slice pepperoni into 18 rounds.

2 Arrange cheese quarters alternately with salami halves, spoke fashion, on top of pizza to make 6 sections; place 2 sausage halves and 2 pepperoni rounds between each near edge. Place 6 pepperoni rounds in a ring in center.

3 Heat, following label directions, or until cheese is bubbly-hot.

4 Place on a large serving tray or platter; cut into 6 wedges; garnish with parsley. Serve with cherry tomatoes.

POULTRY PARADE

Colonial Chicken
Broil 30 minutes. Makes 4 servings

¼ cup buttery-flavor oil
½ teaspoon seasoned salt
¼ teaspoon lemon-pepper seasoning
4 whole chicken breasts, split
1 package (4 ounces) sliced boiled ham
1 can (10½ ounces) chicken gravy
1 can (3 or 4 ounces) sliced mushrooms
1 tablespoon lemon juice

1 Combine oil, salt and pepper seasoning in a cup.

1198

2 Wash and dry chicken breasts; brush both sides with part of oil mixture.
3 Cut ham slices into wide strips.
4 Broil chicken breasts, skin side down, for 15 minutes; turn; brush again.
5 Broil chicken 10 minutes longer. Arrange ham strips on chicken; brush with oil mixture. Broil 5 minutes longer, or until chicken is tender and ham is lightly browned.
6 Heat gravy, mushrooms with liquid and lemon juice until bubbly-hot in a small saucepan.
7 To serve, arrange chicken and ham on small platter; spoon some of gravy mixture over. Serve remaining gravy separately.

Country Chicken Casserole

Bake at 350° for 1 hour and 30 minutes. Makes 6 to 8 servings

2 cans (10½ ounces each) condensed cream
    of mushroom soup
2 cups milk
1 package (8 ounces) uncooked elbow maca-
    roni

3 cans (about 5 ounces each) boned chicken,
    diced
1 package (8 ounces) process American
    cheese, shredded (2 cups)
1 small onion, minced (¼ cup)
4 hard-cooked eggs, shelled and sliced
3 pimientos, drained and chopped
1 teaspoon seasoned salt
⅓ cup grated Parmesan cheese

1 Blend soup and milk until smooth in a 10-cup baking dish. Stir in macaroni, chicken, cheese, onion, eggs, pimientos and salt; cover.
2 Bake in moderate oven (350°) 1 hour and 25 minutes; uncover. Sprinkle with Parmesan cheese. Bake 5 minutes longer, or until cheese is crusty-brown.

1199

Party Chicken

No need to cook all day to enjoy this Southern delicacy—just follow this magic recipe.
Bake at 350° for 30 minutes. Makes 6 to 8 servings

Tomato juice and potato soup layer into an appetizer, package crumbs coat the chicken, a mix makes the cake.

4 chicken legs (drumsticks and thighs)
2 tablespoons all-purpose flour
1 teaspoon salt
⅛ teaspoon pepper
¼ cup vegetable oil
2 packages Spanish-rice mix
1 package (6 to 8 ounces) sliced Italian assortment cold cuts
1 package (5 ounces) frozen cooked deveined shrimps, thawed
2 tablespoons instant chicken bouillon
4 cups hot water

1 Cut chicken legs into drumsticks and thighs; shake in paper bag with flour, salt and pepper to coat evenly.
2 Sauté slowly in vegetable oil in large frying pan 30 minutes, or until fork-tender; place in 10-cup casserole with tight-fitting cover.
3 Sprinkle Spanish rice right from package over chicken; top with sliced meats, then shrimps.
4 Heat chicken bouillon and water to boiling in same frying pan, stirring until bouillon is dissolved; pour over mixture in casserole; cover.
5 Bake in moderate oven (350°) 30 minutes, or until bubbly-hot.

Oven-Crisp Chicken
Onion dip mix gives the crusty crumb coating a zesty flavor lift.
Bake at 350° for 1 hour. Makes 8 servings

2 broiler-fryers (about 2 pounds each), cut up
1 envelope (2 packets) onion dip mix
1 cup soft bread crumbs (2 slices)
1 teaspoon salt
⅛ teaspoon pepper

1 Remove skin from chicken, if you wish; cut away small bones from breast pieces.
2 Combine dip mix, bread crumbs, salt and pepper in a paper bag. Shake chicken pieces, a few at a time, in mixture to coat well. Place, not touching, in a single layer in a well-buttered large shallow baking pan.
3 Bake in moderate oven (350°) 1 hour, or until chicken is tender and richly browned.

A CONTEMPORARY SEAFOOD SAMPLER

Tuna with Mushroom Sauce
Bake at 400° for 20 minutes. Makes 4 servings

2 cans (7 ounces each) tuna, drained and flaked
1 medium-size onion, sliced in thin rings
1 green pepper, sliced in thin strips
2 teaspoons finely chopped parsley
1 can (10½ ounces) cream of mushroom soup
½ soup-can water
½ teaspoon salt
⅛ teaspoon pepper
½ cup shredded process American cheese

1 Grease a 6-cup casserole and in it make layers of tuna, onion, pepper and parsley.
2 Dilute soup with water; add salt and pepper and pour over layers in casserole. Sprinkle cheese over top.
3 Bake approximately 20 minutes in hot oven (400°).

Smorgasbord Tuna Salad
Makes 6 servings

1 can (1 pound) small white potatoes, drained
1 can (1 pound) cut wax beans, drained
6 tablespoons bottled oil-and-vinegar salad dressing
6 large romaine leaves
2 cans (about 7 ounces each) tuna, drained and broken in chunks
1 can (1 pound) tomato wedges, drained
1 tablespoon capers, drained
Freshly ground black pepper

1 Slice potatoes into a medium-size bowl; place beans in a second bowl. Drizzle each with 2 tablespoons of the salad dressing; toss lightly to mix.
2 Line a large salad bowl with romaine; place tuna in center. Pile potatoes, beans and tomatoes in sections around tuna; sprinkle capers over tuna.
3 Drizzle remaining 2 tablespoons salad dressing over tomatoes; sprinkle pepper over all.

Tuna Potpie
Bake at 400° for 12 minutes. Makes 6 servings

3 carrots, sliced
1 small onion, diced (¼ cup)
½ cup sliced celery

1201

¼ cup diced green pepper
1 bay leaf
1 can (10½ ounces) cream of mushroom soup
½ soup-can water
1 can (8 ounces) peas
2 cans (7 ounces each) tuna, drained and flaked
1 package refrigerated biscuits

1 In a medium-size saucepan put the carrots, onion, celery, green pepper and bay leaf, with enough water to barely cover. Bring to boiling and cook until just tender; remove bay leaf; drain. Mix soup and water in a medium-size saucepan; heat until bubbly-hot; add drained vegetables along with peas and tuna. Pour into a greased 6-cup shallow baking dish; top with biscuits. Bake in hot oven (400°) 12 minutes, or until biscuits are golden brown.

Tuna Divan
This busy-day dinner-in-a-dish features tuna and broccoli in a vegetable-soup sauce.
Makes 4 servings

2 packages (10 ounces each) frozen broccoli spears
1 can (10¾ ounces) condensed vegetable soup
¼ cup milk
1 can (about 7 ounces) tuna, drained and flaked
2 tablespoons grated Parmesan cheese

1 Cook broccoli by package directions; drain.
2 Heat soup and milk in small saucepan; beat until smooth.
3 Arrange broccoli in shallow broilerproof dish; top with tuna; pour sauce over; sprinkle with cheese.
4 Slide under broiler, about 4 inches from heat, until bubbly-hot.

Tuna Roly-Poly
Practically everything for this dish is an ''on hand'' from your cupboard shelf.
Bake at 400° about 15 minutes. Makes 4 servings

2 cups biscuit mix
⅔ cup milk
1 can (about 7 ounces) tuna, drained and flaked
1 cup finely diced celery
¼ cup diced stuffed green olives

¼ cup mayonnaise
2 tablespoons dairy sour cream
MUSHROOM SAUCE (recipe follows)

1 Combine biscuit mix and milk in medium-size bowl; mix, following label directions for plain biscuits. Roll or pat out to a rectangle, 8x10, on lightly floured pastry cloth or board.
2 Mix tuna, celery, olives, mayonnaise and sour cream in medium-size bowl; spread evenly over dough. Beginning at one end, roll up, jelly-roll fashion; pinch edges together to seal.
3 Slice crosswise into 8 even-size pieces; place, not touching, on a greased cookie sheet.
4 Bake in hot oven (400°) 15 minutes, or until golden. Serve with MUSHROOM SAUCE.

MUSHROOM SAUCE—Combine 1 can (10½ ounces) condensed cream of mushroom soup and ⅓ cup milk in small saucepan. Heat to boiling; stir in 1 tablespoon cut chives. Makes about 1½ cups.

Salmon Salad Tart
Bake at 450° for 8 minutes, then at 400° for 20 minutes. Makes 8 servings

6 tablespoons (¾ stick) butter or margarine
1½ cups biscuit mix
¼ cup boiling water
2 cans (1 pound each) salmon
3 hard-cooked eggs, shelled
1 cup thinly sliced celery
¼ cup sliced pimiento-stuffed olives
½ cup mayonnaise or salad dressing
1 package (8 ounces) sliced process American cheese

1 Cut butter or margarine into biscuit mix in a medium-size bowl; stir in boiling water until mixture holds together and leaves side of bowl clean. Place in a 9-inch pie plate.
2 Flour hands and dough lightly, then pat out evenly to make a pastrylike shell and line plate completely; flute edge.
3 Bake in very hot oven (450°) 8 minutes, or until golden. Remove from oven and place on a wire rack; cool slightly. Lower oven temperature to hot (400°).
4 Drain liquid from salmon; remove skin and bones. Break salmon into chunks; place in a large bowl. Cut half of 1 egg into wedges to use for garnish; dice remaining eggs and add to salmon with celery, olives and mayonnaise or salad dressing; toss lightly to mix.
5 Cut block of cheese in half diagonally; separate into 8 double triangles; stand around edge in shell. Spoon in salmon mixture. Cover loosely with foil.
6 Bake in hot oven (400°) 20 minutes, or until

1202

Biscuit-mix crust filled with canned salmon + process American cheese + stuffed olives = Salmon Salad Tart.

filling is hot. Garnish with egg wedges. Cut in wedges; serve warm.

●

Stuffed Pancakes Newburg
Makes 6 servings

   2 packages (8 ounces each) frozen pancakes
   2 cups (1 pound) cream-style cottage cheese
   1 small cucumber, pared, seeded, and chopped (⅔ cup)
   1 tablespoon grated onion
   ¼ tablespoon Worcestershire sauce
   ⅛ teaspoon salt
   NEWBURG SHRIMP SAUCE *(recipe follows)*

1 Let pancakes stand in opened package until thawed enough to separate.
2 Combine cottage cheese, cucumber, onion, Worcestershire sauce and salt in medium-size bowl; spread between pancakes to make 6 sandwiches; place on cookie sheet.
3 Bake in moderate oven (350°) 20 to 30 minutes, or until cheese filling is hot; remove from oven; cut in half; serve with NEWBURG SHRIMP SAUCE.

   NEWBURG SHRIMP SAUCE—Combine 1 can (10 ounces) frozen cream of shrimp soup, 1 package (5 ounces) thawed frozen ready-to-eat shrimp, ¼ cup milk and 2 tablespoons chopped parsley in medium-size saucepan; cook over medium heat, stirring often, until smooth and bubbly. Season with 2 teaspoons sherry flavoring, if you wish.

●

Deep-Sea Bake
Unfold each hot foil bundle and the main course of your dinner is ready.
Makes 6 servings

   2 packages (12 ounces each) frozen perch, haddock, cod or flounder fillets
   6 tablespoons (¾ stick) butter or margarine
   1 large onion, chopped (1 cup)
   3 large potatoes, cooked, peeled, and sliced
   2 teaspoons salt
   1 teaspoon paprika
   1 package (10 ounces) frozen whole-kernel corn

1 Cut each package of frozen fish fillets into 3 equal-size servings (no need to thaw).
2 Melt butter or margarine in small saucepan; stir in onion; heat just until bubbly.
3 Have ready six 12-inch squares of heavy aluminum foil. Place about 1 tablespoon butter mixture on each; top with a serving of fish, more

1203

onion-butter mixture then potatoes, dividing evenly. Sprinkle all with salt and paprika; top with frozen corn. Fold and seal foil into bundles with a drugstore wrap.

4 Cook on grill over hot coals, turning every 15 minutes, 1 hour, or until fish flakes easily with a fork. Serve in foil wrappers.

Mandarin Shrimps

Frozen shrimps and vegetables go, Far Eastern fashion, in and out of the frying pan fast.
Makes 6 servings

3 tablespoons vegetable oil
1 bag (1½ pounds) frozen deveined shelled raw shrimps
1 clove of garlic, crushed
1 package (about 10 ounces) frozen green beans and mushrooms
1 can (5 ounces) water chestnuts, drained and sliced
1 can (10½ ounces) condensed chicken broth
¼ teaspoon ground ginger
2 cans (about 11 ounces each) fried rice
2 tablespoons cornstarch
½ cup water
2 tablespoons soy sauce

1 Heat oil quickly in a large frying pan; stir in frozen shrimps and garlic. Sauté 5 minutes; push to one side.
2 Place frozen green beans and mushrooms in pan; heat, breaking vegetables apart as they thaw, 3 minutes; stir in water chestnuts, chicken broth and ginger; cover. Simmer 10 minutes.
3 While shrimp mixture simmers, heat fried rice, following the label directions.
4 Smooth cornstarch and water to a paste in a cup; stir in soy sauce, then stir into shrimp mixture. Cook slowly, stirring constantly, until the mixture thickens and boils 3 minutes.
5 Spoon rice around edge of a large deep serving bowl; spoon shrimp mixture in center. Garnish with sprigs of parsley, if you wish.

1204

Skillet Paella
Makes 6 servings

1 can (1 pound) green peas
1 can (about 5 ounces) boned chicken
1 large onion, chopped (1 cup)
1 clove garlic, chopped
1 tablespoon vegetable oil
2 cups packaged precooked rice
1 can (1 pound) stewed tomatoes
1 can (4 or 5 ounces) Vienna sausages, drained and sliced
¼ teaspoon leaf thyme, crumbled

⅛ teaspoon pepper
2 cans (5 ounces each) deveined shrimps, drained and rinsed

1 Drain liquids from peas and chicken into a 2-cup measure; add water to make 1½ cups. Dice chicken.
2 Sauté onion and garlic in vegetable oil until soft in a large frying pan; stir in rice, tomatoes and the 1½ cups liquid. Heat to boiling; stir in peas, chicken, sausages, thyme and pepper; place shrimps on top; cover.
3 Simmer 10 minutes, or until rice is tender and liquid is absorbed. Just before serving, sprinkle with chopped parsley, if you wish.

Shrimp Salad Silhouettes
Tiny cutout of a contrasting color bread trims each two-bite sandwich.
Makes about 4½ dozen

1 can (5 ounces) deveined shrimps, drained, rinsed and flaked
¾ cup finely chopped celery
¾ cup mayonnaise or salad dressing
1 teaspoon curry powder
1 tablespoon lemon juice
14 slices white bread
14 slices whole-wheat bread
Butter or margarine

1 Mix all ingredients except bread and butter or margarine in a bowl.
2 Place 7 slices each white and whole-wheat bread flat on cutting board; spread with butter or margarine; trim crusts. With a knife, mark each slice into 4 triangles, then cut a small fancy design from each triangle; remove cutouts; place white ones in whole-wheat slices and whole-wheat in white.
3 Spread each of remaining bread slices with butter or margarine; trim crusts; spread with 2 tablespoons shrimp mixture. Put together with cutout slices; cut each into 4 triangles. Wrap and chill.

RICE AND PASTA

Rice Verde
Makes 4 servings

1 package (9 ounces) frozen creamed spinach (in pouch)
Packaged precooked rice

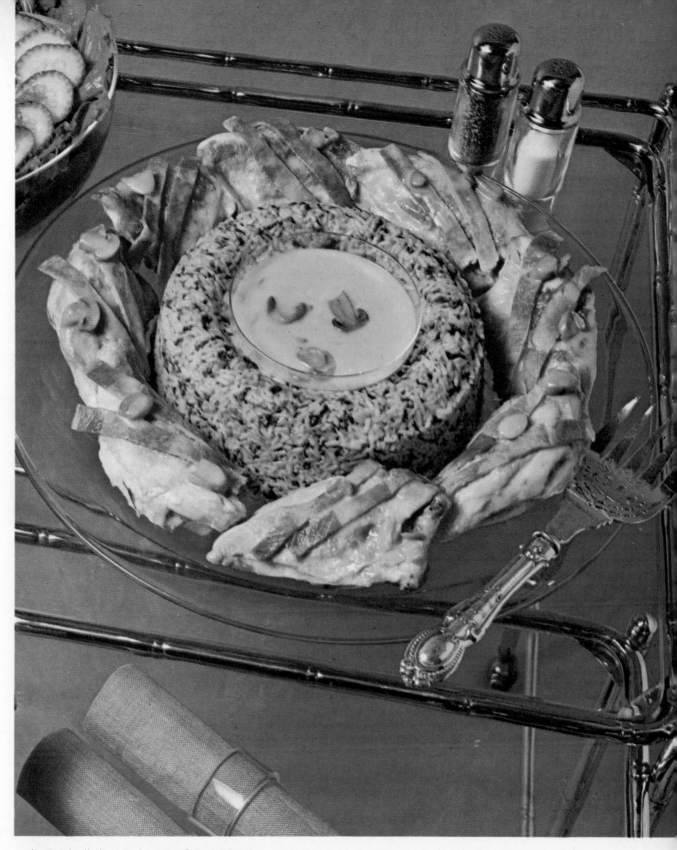

Instant (well almost) elegance: Colonial Chicken, made in half an hour, Rice Verde in just 10 minutes.

Water
Salt
Butter or margarine
Dash of nutmeg

1 Heat spinach, as label directs.
2 Prepare rice with water, salt and butter or margarine, following label directions to make 3 cups.
3 Combine spinach, rice and nutmeg in a large bowl; mixing well. Spoon into a well-buttered 4-cup ring mold. Let stand 5 minutes in a warm place.
4 To unmold, cover ring mold with a heated serving platter; turn both over together; shake gently; lift off mold.

Quick Rice Casserole
Bake at 425° for 10 minutes. Makes 4 servings

  1 package (7 ounces) chicken-flavor rice and vermicelli mix
  2 tablespoons butter or margarine
1¾ cups boiling water

1 Combine rice mix, butter or margarine and boiling water in a 4-cup baking dish. Stir until well blended; cover.
2 Bake in hot oven (425°) for 10 minutes, or until water is absorbed.

Shrimp and Noodles au Gratin
Bake at 350° for 20 minutes. Makes 4 generous servings

  1 package noodles with sour cream and cheese sauce mix
  Milk
  Butter or margarine
  1 package (1 pound) frozen shelled deveined shrimp
  1 can (3 or 4 ounces) sliced mushrooms, drained
  1 carton (8 ounces) cottage cheese
½ teaspoon dillweed
  3 tablespoons fine dry bread crumbs
  1 tablespoon butter or margarine, softened

1 Prepare noodles with milk and butter or margarine in a medium-size saucepan, following label directions.
2 Cook shrimp in a medium-size saucepan, following label directions; drain and chop. Add to noodle mixture.

1206

3 Stir in mushrooms, cottage cheese and dillweed. Spoon into a 6-cup casserole.
4 Combine bread crumbs and butter or margarine in a small bowl. Sprinkle over casserole.
5 Bake in moderate oven (350°) 20 minutes, or until casserole is bubbly-hot.

Spaghetti with Clam Sauce
Friday way with spaghetti—and ready in minutes.
Makes 6 servings

  1 package (1 pound) thin spaghetti
  2 cloves of garlic, minced
½ cup (1 stick) butter or margarine
  4 cans (7 ounces each) minced clams
  2 teaspoons lemon juice
  Dash of cayenne pepper

1 Cook spaghetti, following label directions; drain; keep hot in kettle.
2 While spaghetti cooks, sauté garlic lightly in butter or margarine in medium-size saucepan. Stir in remaining ingredients; simmer 5 minutes.
3 Toss with hot spaghetti; serve plain or with your favorite grated cheese.

Fish-and-Shells Italiano
Flavorful cod and tender macaroni shells bake in a zippy-rich tomato sauce.
Bake at 375° for 30 minutes. Makes 6 servings

  1 package (1 pound) macaroni shells
  1 medium-size onion, chopped (½ cup)
½ teaspoon leaf basil, crumbled
  2 tablespoons olive oil
  1 envelope spaghetti-sauce mix
  1 can (about 2 pounds) Italian tomatoes
  1 package (1 pound) frozen cod fillets, cut into cubes
⅓ cup grated Parmesan cheese
  1 package (8 ounces) sliced mozzarella cheese

1 Cook macaroni shells, following label directions; drain.
2 While shells cook, sauté onion with basil in olive oil in large saucepan; stir in spaghetti-sauce mix and tomatoes. Cover; simmer 10 minutes; add fish cubes; simmer 10 minutes longer.
3 Spoon half the macaroni shells into a 12-cup casserole; sprinkle with half the Parmesan

cheese; top with half the fish-tomato sauce. Repeat layers; arrange mozzarella-cheese slices on top.

4 Bake in moderate oven (375°) 30 minutes, or until bubbly-hot.

Note—If made in the morning and chilled, take from refrigerator and let stand at room temperature 30 minutes before putting into oven to bake.

Macaroni-Tuna Subs

This knife-and-fork whopper starts with ready-to-heat canned macaroni.

Makes 4 servings

2 cans (about 1 pound each) macaroni in cheese sauce
1 can (about 7 ounces) tuna, drained and flaked
2 tablespoons sweet-pickle relish
1 teaspoon Worcestershire sauce
4 toasted split hamburger buns
 Dried chopped parsley

1 Combine macaroni in cheese sauce, tuna, relish and Worcestershire sauce in a medium-size saucepan; heat slowly, stirring often, 5 minutes, or until hot.

2 Spoon over toasted buns; sprinkle with parsley. Serve hot.

Presto Lasagna

The fastest recipe we know for this favorite Italian dish—and it's so good!

Bake at 350° for 30 minutes. Makes 4 servings

1 package (8 ounces) regular noodles
1 tablespoon vegetable oil or olive oil
1 package (8 ounces) heat-and-serve sausage patties
1 can (about 1 pound) Italian tomatoes
1 can (8 ounces) tomato sauce
1 tablespoon instant minced onion
1 teaspoon mixed Italian herbs
1 carton (8 ounces) pot cheese
¼ cup grated Parmesan cheese
1 package (6 or 8 ounces) sliced mozzarella cheese, cut into ½-inch strips

1 Cook noodles, following label directions; drain; return to same kettle; toss with salad oil or olive oil to keep from sticking.

2 While noodles cook, dice sausage patties;

brown with no fat, stirring often, in medium-size frying pan; stir in tomatoes, tomato sauce, onion and herbs; heat to boiling; simmer, stirring often, 5 minutes.

3 Layer half the noodles, pot cheese, Parmesan cheese, tomato mixture and mozzarella cheese in 6-cup shallow baking dish; repeat, criss-crossing mozzarella strips on top.

4 Bake in moderate oven (350°) 30 minutes, or until bubbling at edges and cheese is lightly browned; remove from oven; let stand 5 to 10 minutes to set.

Note—For a party, double the recipe and bake in 12-cup shallow baking dish at 350° until bubbly-hot.

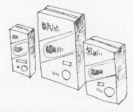

Pinwheel Lasagna

Flexible food, the lasagna noodle! Here you roll it with a two-cheese filling.

Bake at 350° for 45 minutes. Makes 6 servings

12 lasagne noodles (from a 1-pound package)
2 cups (1-pound carton) cream-style cottage cheese
1 package (3 or 4 ounces) cream cheese
2 eggs
¼ cup chopped parsley
1 teaspoon leaf basil, crumbled
½ teaspoon salt
1 jar (1 pound) meatless spaghetti sauce
1 package (8 ounces) sliced mozzarella or pizza cheese

1 Slide lasagne noodles, one at a time, into a kettle of boiling salted water. Cook, following label directions; drain; return to kettle. Cover with cold water.

2 Combine cottage and cream cheeses in a medium-size bowl; beat in eggs, parsley, basil and salt.

3 Lift noodles, one at a time, from water; drain on paper toweling. Spread with ¼ cup of the cheese filling; roll up, jelly-roll fashion.

4 Place, seam-side down, in a large shallow baking dish; spoon spaghetti sauce over rolls; cover dish.

5 Bake in moderate oven (350°) 40 minutes; uncover. Cut mozzarella or pizza cheese into strips; arrange over rolls in dish. Bake 5 minutes longer, or until cheese melts.

1207

A DOZEN QUICK-TO-FIX VEGETABLE DISHES

Casserole Creamed Vegetables
Bake at 375° for 1 hour. Makes 8 servings

2 packages (9 ounces each) frozen French fried potatoes
Boiling water
2 packages (9 ounces each) frozen cut green beans
1 can (3½ ounces) French fried onions
1 can (10½ ounces) condensed cream of mushroom soup
⅔ cup milk
2 tablespoons chopped pimientos
½ teaspoon salt
⅛ teaspoon pepper

1 Place frozen potatoes in a strainer; pour boiling water over top; drain well. Pile in center of a greased deep 12-cup baking dish.
2 Place frozen beans in strainer; pour boiling water over top; drain well. Mix with half of the onions in a medium-size bowl; spoon around edge in baking dish.
3 Blend mushroom soup with milk, pimientos, salt and pepper in a small bowl; pour over vegetable mixture; cover.
4 Bake in moderate oven (375°) 55 minutes; uncover. Sprinkle remaining onions over top. Bake 5 minutes longer, or until vegetables are tender and onions are hot.

Duchess Vegetables
Bake at 375° for 40 minutes. Makes 6 servings

3 cups prepared instant mashed potatoes
1 can (1 pound) sliced carrots, drained
2 cans (1 pound each) cut green beans, drained
Salt
Pepper
½ teaspoon leaf marjoram, crumbled
3 tablespoons butter or margarine

1 Spoon mashed potatoes into a 9-inch pie plate, building up edge to form a shell.
2 Place carrots in a row across middle in shell; spoon green beans on each side; sprinkle with salt, pepper and marjoram. Dot with butter or margarine. Cover loosely with foil.
3 Bake in moderate oven (375°) 40 minutes, or until vegetables are hot.

Savory Oven Vegetables
Bake at 425° for 30 minutes. Makes 4 servings

1 package (10 ounces) frozen mixed vegetables
2 tablespoons butter or margarine
2 tablespoons water
½ teaspoon salt
½ teaspoon dillweed

1 Combine frozen mixed vegetables, butter or margarine, water, salt, and dillweed in a 4-cup baking dish; cover.
2 Bake in hot oven (425°) 30 minutes, or until tender, stirring once to blend seasonings.

Creole Succotash
The beans blend deliciously with golden corn and ready-seasoned stewed tomatoes.
Makes 6 servings

1 package (10 ounces) frozen baby lima beans
1 package (10 ounces) frozen whole-kernel corn
1 can (about 1 pound) stewed tomatoes
3 tablespoons butter or margarine

1 Cook lima beans, following label directions; when almost tender, add corn; heat to boiling; simmer 2 minutes. (If needed, add 1 or 2 tablespoons water to finish cooking, but when done, water should be absorbed.)
2 Stir in tomatoes; heat just until steaming hot; spoon succotash into serving dishes and top each with a pat of butter or margarine.

Green Bean Medley
Makes 4 servings

1 package (9 ounces) frozen Italian green beans
Water
Salt
1 can (8 ounces) small boiled onions, drained
¼ cup chopped pimiento
2 tablespoons chopped parsley
1 tablespoon butter or margarine
½ teaspoon salt
⅛ teaspoon pepper
⅛ teaspoon garlic powder

1 Cook green beans with water and salt, following label directions, in a medium-size saucepan. Drain.
2 Combine green beans with pimiento, parsley,

butter or margarine, salt, pepper and garlic powder in same saucepan. Heat until bubbly-hot.

Milano Potato Mold
Bake at 350° for 1 hour. Makes 6 to 8 servings

2 tablespoons fine dry bread crumbs
Instant mashed potatoes
Water
Butter or margarine
Salt
2 eggs
¼ cup grated Parmesan cheese
2 tablespoons chopped parsley
⅛ teaspoon pepper
4 slices provolone cheese (from an 8-ounce package)

1 Butter a 6-cup ovenproof bowl; coat lightly with bread crumbs.
2 Prepare enough instant mashed potatoes with water, butter or margarine and salt (*omit milk*), following label directions, to make 3 cups. Beat in eggs, 1 at a time; stir in Parmesan cheese, parsley and pepper.
3 Spoon one third into prepared bowl; top with 2 slices of the provolone cheese. Repeat layers; spoon remaining potato mixture on top.
4 Bake in moderate oven (350°) 1 hour, or until golden and potatoes start to pull away from side of bowl. Cool in bowl on a wire rack 10 minutes. Loosen mold around edge with a knife; tip and shake bowl gently to loosen mold from bottom; invert onto a heated serving plate; lift off bowl. Serve hot.

Potatoes Delmonico
It's amazing how fast you can make this classic potato recipe with new products.
Bake at 350° about 45 minutes. Makes 6 to 8 servings

9 cups water
1 teaspoon salt
1 package (8 ounces) dehydrated sliced potatoes (4½ cups)
1 can (about 11 ounces) chicken gravy
1 tablespoon grated onion
1 teaspoon dry mustard
1 teaspoon paprika
¼ teaspoon pepper
1¼ cups milk

2 packages (4 ounces each) shredded Cheddar cheese (2 cups)
2 pimientos, diced

1 Heat water to boiling in large saucepan; add salt and potatoes; cover; lower heat; cook 20 minutes.
2 While potatoes cook, combine chicken gravy, onion, mustard, paprika and pepper in 4-cup measure; gradually stir in milk.
3 Drain potatoes; place in baking dish, 13x9x3; sprinkle with cheese and pimientos; toss to mix; pour gravy mixture over; cover with foil.
4 Bake in moderate oven (350°) 45 minutes, or until bubbly-hot in the middle.

Parisian Potato Puff
Distinctive differences for the instant variety: Gruyère, onion, green pepper.
Bake at 375° for 20 minutes. Makes 6 servings

2 tablespoons chopped green pepper
2 tablespoons chopped green onion
1 tablespoon bacon drippings
4 cups prepared instant mashed potatoes
1 package (6 ounces) process Gruyère cheese, cut in small cubes
¼ cup bacon-flavor bits

1 Sauté green pepper and onion in bacon drippings until soft in a small frying pan; beat into mashed potatoes. Fold in three fourths of the cheese.
2 Spoon mixture into a 4-cup baking dish; sprinkle remaining cheese over top.
3 Bake in moderate oven (375°) 20 minutes, or until cheese melts and potatoes are lightly golden. Sprinkle bacon bits over top.

Skillet Potato Medley
For a change, brown frozen French fries, add seasoned tomatoes, and simmer.
Makes 6 to 8 servings

1 large onion, chopped (1 cup)
1 cup chopped celery
3 tablespoons vegetable oil
1 bag (2 pounds) frozen French fried potatoes
2 teaspoons salt
¼ teaspoon pepper
1 can (about 1 pound) stewed tomatoes
1 tablespoon chopped parsley

1 Sauté onion and celery in vegetable oil until soft in a large frying pan. Stir in frozen potatoes; sprinkle salt and pepper over top. Cook slowly, stirring several times, until potatoes are golden.
2 Pour tomatoes and juice over potato mixture; stir lightly; cover. Heat slowly, stirring once or twice, until almost all liquid is absorbed. Spoon into a heated serving bowl; sprinkle with chopped parsley. Serve with broiled hamburger patties or steak.

Skillet Potato Pie
Hearty with eggs, bacon and potatoes, it's an ideal main dish for breakfast, lunch or supper.
Makes 6 servings

6 slices bacon, cut up
1 medium-size onion, peeled and sliced
1 package (9 ounces) frozen French fried potatoes
6 eggs
⅓ cup milk
1 teaspoon salt
Paprika

1 Sauté bacon until crisp in a large frying pan; drain on paper toweling and set aside for Step 3.
2 Cook onion with frozen potatoes in same pan, following label directions for pan-frying. Pour all fat from pan.
3 Beat eggs with milk and salt in a medium-size bowl; pour over potatoes and onion; sprinkle with cooked bacon and paprika; cover.
4 Cook over low heat 15 minutes, or until eggs are set. Cut in wedges.

French-Fry Bake
Bake at 350° for 45 minutes. Makes 6 servings

5 slices bacon
2 tablespoons all-purpose flour
¼ teaspoon salt
¼ teaspoon pepper
2½ cups milk
1 tablespoon instant minced onion
1 teaspoon Worcestershire sauce
1 package (8 ounces) sliced process American cheese, cut up
3 packages (9 ounces each) frozen French fried potatoes

1 Sauté bacon until crisp in a medium-size frying pan; drain.

2 Pour off all fat, then measure 3 tablespoonfuls and return to pan; stir in flour, salt, and pepper. Cook, stirring constantly, until bubbly. Stir in milk, onion, and Worcestershire sauce; continue cooking and stirring until sauce thickens and boils 1 minute. Stir in cheese.
3 Pour over frozen potatoes in a baking dish, 13x9x2; toss to mix well. Crumble bacon on top.
4 Bake in moderate oven (350°) 45 minutes, or until bubbly-hot.

Onions Mornay
For serving, spoon the creamy sauce over the toasty bread—what good eating!
Bake at 350° for 30 minutes. Makes 6 servings

4 tablespoons (½ stick) butter or margarine
2 large sweet onions, coarsely chopped (4 cups)
2 cloves garlic, minced
1 can (10½ ounces) condensed cream of celery soup
1 cup milk
¼ teaspoon seasoned pepper
1 can (1 pound) cut green beans, drained
2 packages (8 ounces each) sliced process Swiss cheese
12 half-inch-thick slices French bread

1 Melt butter or margarine in a large frying pan; stir in onions and garlic; cover. Cook 15 minutes; stir in soup, milk and pepper; heat, stirring several times, until bubbly.
2 Make two layers each of beans, cheese slices and sauce in a buttered 8-cup baking dish; arrange bread slices, overlapping, on top.
3 Bake in moderate oven (350°) 30 minutes, or until bubbly-hot.

SOME SALAD BOWL SLEIGHT OF HAND

Crab Salad
Serve as an appetizer, California style, or spoon into lettuce cups for a main-dish salad.
Makes 4 servings

1 package (about 6 ounces) frozen king crabmeat, thawed and drained
½ cup diced celery
2 tablespoons bottled Italian-style dressing
4 dashes liquid red pepper seasoning
    Parsley
4 lemon wedges

1 Cut crabmeat into medium-size chunks,
carefully removing any bony tissue; combine
with celery in a small bowl.
2 Sprinkle with salad dressing and pepper seasoning; toss to mix well.
3 Serve in small scallop-shell-shape dishes or
salad plates; garnish with parsley and a lemon
wedge.
Note—Double this recipe for a main-dish salad
to be served in lettuce cups.

●

Western Salmon Salad Bowl
Golden pineapple tidbits add sparkle to this
West Coast favorite.
Makes 4 servings

1 can (1 pound) salmon
1 can (9 ounces) pineapple tidbits, drained
1½ cups chopped celery
2 tablespoons grated onion
2 tablespoons lemon juice
    Few drops bottled red pepper seasoning
    OLD-FASHIONED BOILED DRESSING (recipe fol-
    lows)
1 small head iceberg lettuce
    Lemon wedges

1 Drain salmon; flake into large pieces, removing any small bones and skin.
2 Combine pineapple tidbits, celery, onion,
lemon juice, red pepper seasoning and ½ cup
OLD-FASHIONED BOILED DRESSING in medium-size
bowl. Fold in flaked salmon; cover; chill.
3 Edge salad bowl with a few lettuce leaves;
chop remaining lettuce and place in bottom.
Spoon salad mixture on top; garnish with lemon
wedges. Pass remaining dressing.
    OLD-FASHIONED BOILED DRESSING—Mix 2 table-
spoons flour, 1 tablespoon sugar, 1 teaspoon
salt, 1 teaspoon dry mustard, ¼ teaspoon
ground ginger and a dash of cayenne in top
of double boiler. Beat in ¾ cup milk and 1 egg
until well blended. Cook over simmering water,
stirring constantly, 10 minutes, or until mixture
thickens. Remove from heat; gradually blend in
¼ cup cider vinegar. Pour into a small bowl;
cover; chill. Makes about 1 cup.

First class accompaniments from convenience foods.

German Potato Salad

This old-fashioned winner goes modern with quick-fix potatoes and lots of crisp bacon chips in a hot spicy dressing.
Makes 6 servings

½ pound (about 12 slices) bacon, cut in ½-inch pieces
1 package (1 pound) frozen French fried potatoes
1 cup chopped celery
2 tablespoons cider vinegar
2 tablespoons brown sugar
½ teaspoon salt
Dash of pepper

1 Sauté bacon until crisp in a large frying pan; drain on paper toweling.
2 Cook potatoes in same pan, following label directions for pan-frying; drain on paper toweling. Cut into bite-size pieces and combine with bacon and celery in a salad bowl.
3 Pour off all drippings, then measure 2 tablespoonfuls and return to pan; stir in remaining ingredients. Heat to boiling; then simmer 1 minute. Pour over potato mixture; toss to mix well. Serve warm.

Hungarian Bean Bowl

Red and white kidney beans dressed with peppy seasoned sour cream make this unusual casserole-salad.
Makes 6 to 8 servings

1 can (about 1 pound) red kidney beans
1 can (about 1 pound) white kidney beans
2 tablespoons vegetable oil
2 tablespoons cider vinegar
2 tablespoons chopped parsley
2 teaspoons sugar
1 envelope garlic-olive dip mix
1 small head of iceberg lettuce, shredded
½ cup dairy sour cream
1 can (about 3 ounces) French fried onion rings

1 Drain red and white kidney beans well; place beans in a large bowl.
2 Drizzle with vegetable oil and vinegar; sprinkle with parsley, sugar and dip mix; toss to mix well. Cover; chill at least an hour to season and blend flavors. (Or let stand at room temperature if you prefer salad not too chilled.)
3 When ready to serve, place shredded lettuce

1212

in a large casserole or bowl. Stir sour cream into bean mixture; spoon on top of lettuce; sprinkle with onion rings.

Yankee Doddle Salad

Popular macaroni and cheese with a new twist —and a main dish and salad in one.
Makes 4 servings

1 can (about 1 pound) macaroni in cheese sauce
½ pound unsliced bologna, cubed
1 cup sliced celery
½ cup chopped sweet pickles
2 tablespoons mayonnaise
1 teaspoon dry mustard
1 head iceberg lettuce, quartered

1 Combine all ingredients, except lettuce, in medium-size bowl; toss lightly with a fork to mix. (If made ahead, chill until serving time.)
2 Spoon generously over lettuce wedges. Serve plain or with sliced tomatoes, if you wish.

Marinated Bean and Chestnut Bowl

Makes 4 servings

1 can (1 pound) sliced green beans, drained
¼ cup sliced water chestnuts
½ cup halved cherry tomatoes
½ cup oil and vinegar dressing
2 teaspoons minced onion
1 teaspoon parsley flakes
½ teaspoon leaf basil, crumbled
1 small head iceberg lettuce

1 Combine beans, water chestnuts and halved tomatoes in a medium-size bowl.
2 Combine dressing, onion, parsley and basil in a jar with a tight lid; cover; shake until well blended.
3 Pour dressing over vegetables; cover. Marinate in refrigerator 3 hours.
4 Break lettuce into a salad bowl.
5 Drain vegetables; spoon into lettuce-lined bowl.

Salad Corn Mingle

Makes 8 servings

2 cans (12 ounces each) Mexican-style corn
1 can (1 pound) Italian green beans

5 large radishes, trimmed
  and chopped
½ cup mayonnaise or salad dressing
2 tablespoons sweet-pickle relish, drained
1 teaspoon lemon juice
½ teaspoon salt
  Iceberg lettuce

1 Drain liquids from corn and beans; combine vegetables with radishes in a medium-size bowl.
2 Blend mayonnaise or salad dressing, pickle relish, lemon juice and salt in a small bowl; fold into vegetable mixture. Serve in a lettuce-lined bowl.

Lima Salad Cups
They double as a vegetable, travel well, need no chilling
Makes 6 servings

2 packages (10 ounces each) frozen Fordhook
  lima beans
2 cups sliced celery
¼ cup thin French dressing
¼ pound unsliced process American cheese,
  cut in small cubes
1 pimiento, diced
  Lettuce

1 Cook lima beans, following label directions, adding celery during last 5 minutes' cooking; drain; place in medium-size bowl.
2 Pour French dressing over; toss lightly to mix; cool.
3 Just before serving, add cheese and pimiento; toss lightly. Serve in lettuce-lined cups or bowls.

Spinach Salad Imperial
Makes 8 servings

1 package (10 ounces) fresh spinach
¼ pound sliced maple-flavor bacon, cut in 1-
  inch pieces
1 large carrot, pared and shredded
⅓ cup bottled oil-and-vinegar salad dressing
4 slices process white American cheese, cut
  in small squares
1 cup onion-ring snacks

1 Trim stems and any coarse ribs from spinach. Wash leaves and drain well. Break or cut into bite-size pieces; place in a large salad bowl.

2 Sauté bacon until crisp in a medium-size frying pan; remove and drain on paper toweling.
3 Just before serving, add carrot to spinach; drizzle dressing over top; toss lightly to mix. Stack cheese and bacon in center; sprinkle onion rings over all.

Grapefruit-Cucumber Toss
Makes 4 servings

4 cups broken romaine
2 cups broken endive
1 small cucumber
2 cups drained unsweetened grapefruit sections (from a 32-ounce jar)
½ cup bottled Russian dressing

1 Arrange greens in a salad bowl.
2 Score cucumber and slice thin; arrange on top of lettuce in a ring; spoon grapefruit sections in center.
3 Just before serving, drizzle dressing over; toss to coat well.

Wilted Cabbage Slaw
Makes 4 servings

4 cups shredded cabbage (½ small head)
1 cup shredded carrot (1 large)
½ cup sliced celery
1 small onion, sliced
1 envelope Italian salad dressing mix
  Vinegar
  Water
  Vegetable oil

1 Combine cabbage, carrot, celery and sliced onion in a medium-size bowl.
2 Prepare salad dressing mix with vinegar, water and oil, following label directions.
3 Heat ½ cup of the prepared dressing just to boiling; pour over vegetables; toss lightly. Refrigerate remaining dressing to use for salads at other meals.

Buffet Mold
Makes 6 to 8 servings

2 envelopes unflavored gelatin
2¾ cups cold water
1 can (6 ounces) frozen concentrated orange
  juice
¼ cup sugar
⅛ teaspoon salt

2 tablespoons lemon juice
½ cup shredded carrot
½ cup finely chopped celery
1 cup cottage cheese
1 can (9 ounces) crushed pineapple, drained

1 Soften gelatin in ½ cup cold water in top of double boiler; dissolve over hot water; remove from heat.
2 Stir in orange juice, 2¼ cups water, sugar, salt and lemon juice; divide in half; chill one half until syrupy; keep other half at room temperature for Step 4.
3 Fold carrot and celery into syrupy gelatin; pour into 6-cup mold; chill until almost set. (Gelatin layer should be slightly sticky so second layer will mold to it as it chills.)
4 Chill second half of gelatin until syrupy; fold in cottage cheese and pineapple; spoon carefully on top of almost-firm gelatin; chill 2 to 3 hours, or until firm. Unmold; serve plain or with dressing.

Grapefruit-Aspic Mold
Makes 6 servings

2 cans (1 pound each) grapefruit sections
    Water
1 package (6 ounces) lemon-flavor gelatin
2 cans (8 ounces each) tomato sauce
    Few drops liquid red pepper seasoning

1 Drain syrup from grapefruit into a 2-cup measure. (Set grapefruit aside for Step 3.) Add water to syrup to make 2 cups; heat to boiling in small saucepan.
2 Pour over gelatin in a medium-size bowl, stirring until gelatin dissolves. Stir in tomato sauce and liquid red pepper seasoning until well blended. Chill about 30 minutes, or until as thick as unbeaten egg white.
3 Fold in grapefruit sections; spoon into a 6-cup mold. Chill several hours, or until firm.
4 To unmold, run a sharp-tip thin-blade knife around top of mold, then dip mold *very quickly* in and out of a pan of hot water. Cover mold with serving plate; turn upside down; carefully lift off mold.
5 Serve plain as a relish, or as a salad garnished with watercress or small inner leaves of romaine. Pass your favorite mayonnaise or salad dressing in a separate bowl.

1214

BREADS AND SANDWICHES

Corn Pillows
Bake at 425° for 12 minutes. Makes 24 little rolls

1 package (10 ounces) corn-bread mix
¾ cup sifted all-purpose flour
1 teaspoon salt
1 teaspoon baking powder
½ teaspoon barbecue spice
¾ cup dairy sour cream
1 egg, beaten
1 roll (6 ounces) hickory-flavor process cheese food

1 Mix corn-bread mix, flour, salt, baking powder and barbecue spice in a large bowl. Stir in sour cream and egg until mixture forms a stiff dough that leaves side of bowl clean. Form into a ball; divide in half.
2 Roll out dough, half at a time, ¼ inch thick on a lightly floured pastry cloth or board; cut into rounds with a floured 3-inch cookie cutter.
3 Cut 12 quarter-inch-thick slices from cheese; cut each in half. (Chill remaining cheese for a snack or sandwich.) Place a cheese crescent on half of each circle of dough; fold dough over to cover cheese; press edges together with a fork to seal. Place on a lightly greased large cookie sheet.
4 Bake in hot oven (425°) 12 minutes, or until rolls are firm and golden. Remove from cookie sheet to wire racks. Serve warm.

Cheese 'n' Bacon Corn Bread
Cut this savory bread into squares and serve hot right from its pan.
Bake at 400° for 25 minutes. Makes 1 loaf

1 package corn muffin mix
½ cup shredded sharp Cheddar cheese
6 slices bacon, cooked and crumbled
1 egg
    Milk

1 Empty corn muffin mix into a medium-size bowl. Save about 1 tablespoon each cheese and bacon for topping; stir remaining into muffin mix.
2 Mix in egg and milk, following label directions; pour into greased baking pan, 8x8x2.
3 Bake in hot oven (400°) 15 minutes; sprinkle saved cheese and bacon on top; bake 10 minutes longer, or until firm and richly golden.

Spoon Bread

Bake at 325° for 1 hour and 25 minutes. Makes 6 servings

3 eggs
2 cups milk
2 tablespoons butter or margarine, melted
1 package corn-bread mix

1 Beat eggs well in a medium-size bowl; beat in milk, butter or margarine and corn-bread mix until smooth with a rotary beater. Pour into a greased 6-cup baking dish.
2 Bake in slow oven (325°) 1 hour and 25 minutes, or until firm and golden.
3 Serve at once in place of potatoes with butter or margarine or gravy.

Cheddar Biscuits

Bake at 425° for 10 minutes. Makes 12 biscuits

2 cups biscuit mix
¾ cup shredded sharp Cheddar cheese
3 tablespoons bacon-flavor bits
Milk

1 Combine biscuit mix, cheese and bacon bits in a large bowl; add milk, following label directions, stirring just until mixture is moist.
2 Turn dough out onto a lightly floured pastry cloth or board; knead 8 to 10 times. Roll out ½ inch thick; cut into rounds with a 2-inch biscuit cutter. Place on a large cookie sheet.
3 Bake in hot oven (425°) 10 minutes, or until puffed and golden. Serve hot.

Biscuit Crisps

Each triangle is thin, crisp and butter-rich.
Bake at 400° about 5 minutes. Makes about 6½ dozen triangles

1 package refrigerated plain or buttermilk biscuits
3 tablespoons melted butter or margarine
Sesame seeds

1 Separate biscuits; roll out each into a 5-inch round on an ungreased cookie sheet (one sheet holds 4 rounds); brush lightly with melted butter or margarine; sprinkle with sesame seeds; cut each round into eighths with pastry wheel or sharp knife.
2 Bake in hot oven (400°) 5 minutes, or just until golden; remove from cookie sheet at once with pancake turner or broad spatula; repeat with remaining biscuits, washing cookie sheet each time to keep the crisps from sticking to it.
3 Cool completely on wire racks; store in container with tight-fitting cover.

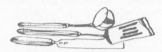

Sandwich-in-the-Round

Meat, cheese, potato salad and relish extras on a speedy biscuit crust make this "hot" headliner for a cool summery meal.
Bake at 450° for 10 minutes. Makes 6 servings

2 packages refrigerated plain or buttermilk biscuits
Butter or margarine
1 jar (1 pound) potato salad
6 slices big bologna
Parsley
4 slices provolone cheese (from 8-ounce package)
3 slices big salami
6 long dill pickle strips
1 small cucumber, sliced thin
2 medium-size tomatoes, cut in wedges
2 hard-cooked eggs, sieved
12 thin radish slices
Ripe olives
RUSSIAN DRESSING (recipe follows)

1 Place refrigerated biscuits in single layer in bottom of ungreased 14-inch pizza pan; flatten and press together with fingers to cover bottom of pan.
2 Bake in very hot oven (450°) 10 minutes, or until golden. Spread generously with butter or margarine.
3 While crust bakes, spoon about 3 tablespoons potato salad on each bologna slice; roll up; tuck sprigs of parsley in ends. Stack provolone and salami, alternating slices; cut into 6 wedges.
4 When ready to serve, arrange dill-pickle strips, spoke fashion, on top of hot crust to make 6 sections. Place a bologna roll at curved edge and a cheese-and-salami wedge at pointed end of each. Overlap cucumber slices and tomato wedges in between, then spoon sieved egg behind meat-and-cheese wedges.
5 Garnish each cheese wedge with two interlocking radish slices; place a ripe olive in center.
6 To serve, cut into 6 wedges; pass RUSSIAN DRESSING to spoon over.
    RUSSIAN DRESSING—Blend ½ cup mayonnaise or salad dressing and ¼ cup bottled chili sauce in small bowl; cover; chill. Makes ¾ cup.

1215

Cheese-Stuffed Rye Round
Bake at 350° for 20 minutes.

1 one-pound round loaf rye bread
1 package (4 ounces) shredded Cheddar cheese

1 Divide rye bread into quarters, cutting almost to but not through bottom crust. Cut each quarter into slices, again cutting almost to but not through the crust.
2 Sprinkle cheese between each slice of bread. Wrap loaf tightly in foil.
3 Bake in moderate oven (350°) for 20 minutes, or until cheese is melted.

Golden Herb-Cheese Bread
Bake at 375° for 40 to 45 minutes. Makes 1 loaf

¼ cup grated Parmesan cheese
¼ cup minced parsley
¼ teaspoon leaf basil, crumbled
¼ teaspoon leaf oregano, crumbled
1 package hot-roll mix
   Yellow cornmeal
2 tablespoons melted butter or margarine

1 Stir cheese, parsley and herbs into hot-roll mix; make into dough, following label directions for bread; knead; let rise; knead again; shape into loaf, following label directions.
2 Place in loaf pan, 9x5x2½, greased and sprinkled lightly with cornmeal; let rise until double in bulk; make gashes across top 1½ inches deep; brush with melted butter or margarine; sprinkle with more cornmeal.
3 Bake in moderate oven (375°) 40 to 45 minutes, or until firm.

1216

Sesame Whirls
After roast comes from the oven, turn up the heat to bake these little dinner breads.
Bake at 375° for 12 minutes. Makes 16 rolls

2 tablespoons sesame seeds
4 tablespoons (½ stick) butter or margarine, melted
2 packages refrigerated swirl dinner rolls

1 Place sesame seeds in a small frying pan;

heat very slowly, shaking pan constantly, until seeds are lightly toasted. Spoon seeds and melted butter or margarine, dividing evenly, into 16 medium-size muffin-pan cups.
2 Separate the 8 rolls in each package; press, one at a time, into muffin-pan cups, then turn seed side up.
3 Bake in moderate oven (375°) 12 minutes, or until golden; remove from pans. Serve hot.

Mantilla Braid
Bake at 375° for 20 minutes. Makes 8 servings

1 package refrigerated crescent rolls
1 jar (about 5 ounces) bacon-cheese spread
16 pimiento-stuffed olives, halved
1 tablespoon cream
1 tablespoon sesame seeds

1 Unroll crescent-roll dough into two rectangles; place, with sides slightly overlapping, on a large cookie sheet. Set cookie sheet on a damp towel to prevent slipping, then roll dough to a rectangle, 14x8.
2 Spread cheese in a 2-inch-wide strip down center of dough; place halved olives over cheese.
3 Make cuts in dough, 1 inch apart, from outer edges almost to filling; fold strips, alternating from side to side, across filling at an angle. Brush braid with cream; sprinkle with sesame seeds.
4 Bake in moderate oven (375°) 20 minutes, or until golden. Cut into slices; serve hot.

Pecan-Date Ring
Brown-sugar—nut syrup gives a homemade touch to popular date-bread mix.
Bake at 350° for 40 minutes. Makes one 8-inch ring

½ cup (1 stick) butter or margarine
½ cup firmly packed brown sugar
½ teaspoon vanilla
½ cup pecans, slivered
1 package date-bread mix
   Egg
   Water

1 Melt butter or margarine in a small saucepan;

remove from heat. Stir in brown sugar and vanilla.

2 Sprinkle pecans into a greased 7-cup ring mold; carefully pour brown-sugar syrup over pecans.

3 Prepare date-bread mix with egg and water, following label directions; spoon over pecan mixture in mold.

4 Bake in moderate oven (350°) 40 minutes, or until a wooden pick inserted near center comes out clean. Let stand 10 minutes in mold on a wire rack; invert onto a serving plate. Serve warm or cold.

Lemon-Walnut Bread
Bake at 350° for 55 minutes. Makes 1 loaf, 8x4x2

1 *package lemon muffin mix*
  Egg
  Milk
¾ *cup chopped walnuts*
2 *tablespoons sugar*
½ *teaspoon ground cinnamon*
1 *tablespoon butter or margarine, melted*

1 Prepare muffin mix with egg and milk, following label directions; stir in ½ cup of the walnuts. Spoon into a greased loaf pan, 8x4x2.

2 Mix sugar, cinnamon, melted butter or margarine and remaining ¼ cup walnuts in a small bowl; sprinkle evenly over batter.

3 Bake in moderate oven (350°) 55 minutes, or until golden and a wooden pick inserted in center comes out clean. Cool in pan on a wire rack 10 minutes. Loosen around edges with a knife; turn out onto rack. Sprinkle with grated lemon peel, if you wish; let loaf cool completely.

4 Wrap in wax paper, foil or transparent wrap. Store overnight to mellow flavors and make slicing easier. Cut in thin slices.

Steamed Ginger Brown Bread
Makes 2 loaves

1 *package gingerbread mix*
¼ *cup yellow cornmeal*
1 *teaspoon salt*
1½ *cups milk*
1 *cup seedless raisins*

1 Combine gingerbread mix, cornmeal and salt in a large bowl; stir in milk until mixture is evenly moist, then beat at medium speed of electric mixer 2 minutes; stir in raisins.

2 Pour batter into two greased 1-pound coffee cans; cover with foil; fasten with string to hold tightly.

3 Place cans on a rack or trivet in a kettle or steamer; pour in boiling water to half the depth of cans; cover.

4 Steam 3 hours, or until bread is firm and a long skewer inserted in center comes out clean. (Keep water boiling gently during entire cooking time, adding more boiling water, if needed.)

5 Cool bread in cans on a wire rack 5 minutes. Loosen around edges with a knife; turn out onto rack; cool. Slice and serve warm or cold.

Blueberry Ring
Coffeecake at its easiest blends lemon with muffin mix.
Bake at 375° for 40 minutes. Makes 1 large round loaf

2 *packages blueberry muffin mix*
2 *teaspoons grated lemon peel*
2 *eggs*
1 *cup milk*
3 *tablespoons light corn syrup*
2 *tablespoons lemon juice*

1 Grease an 8-cup tube mold.

2 Combine muffin mix and lemon peel in a large bowl; stir in eggs and milk, following label directions. Spoon into prepared mold.

3 Bake in moderate oven (375°) 40 minutes, or until a wooden pick inserted near center comes out clean. Cool in mold on a wire rack 10 minutes; loosen around side and tube with a knife; invert onto a plate.

4 Mix corn syrup and lemon juice in a cup; spoon over warm cake to glaze lightly; cool cake completely.

Sugared Apricot Miniatures
Snowy snack-size loaves bake in your individual gelatin molds.
Bake at 350° for 35 minutes. Makes 8 small loaves

1 *package apricot-nut bread mix*
½ *teaspoon ground cinnamon*
1 *egg*

1217

1 cup pineapple juice
1 teaspoon vanilla
    10X (confectioners' powdered) sugar

1 Grease 8 individual gelatin molds.
2 Combine nut-bread mix and cinnamon in a large bowl; add egg, pineapple juice and vanilla; mix, following label directions. Spoon into prepared molds, filling each about ¾ full. Set molds, not touching, in a jelly-roll pan for ease in handling.
3 Bake in moderate oven (350°) 35 minutes, or until centers spring back when lightly pressed with fingertip. Cool in molds on wire racks 10 minutes. Loosen around edges with a knife; turn out onto racks; cool completely. Sprinkle lightly with 10X sugar and garnish each with a dried apricot and walnut half, if you wish.

Strawberry Puffins
Their delicate fruit flavor comes from a can of instant drink mix.
Bake at 400° for 10 minutes. Makes 3½ dozen small muffins

½ cup strawberry-flavor drink mix
¾ cup milk
1 egg
2 tablespoons vegetable oil
2 cups biscuit mix
    10X (confectioners' powdered) sugar

1 Combine drink mix, milk, egg and oil in a small bowl; beat with fork until well blended.
2 Add all at once to biscuit mix in medium-size bowl; stir just until biscuit mix is completely moistened. (Batter will be soft.)
3 Spoon into greased tiny muffin-pan cups (about 1¾ x ¾ inches), filling each two-thirds full.
4 Bake in hot oven (400°) 10 minutes, or until delicately golden but not browned.
5 Remove from pans; sprinkle tops with 10X sugar, serve hot.

1218

DESSERT MAGIC FROM MIXES

February Shortcake
Bake at 450° for 15 minutes. Makes 8 servings

2 packages refrigerated buttermilk biscuits
1 cup sifted all-purpose flour
½ cup firmly packed light brown sugar

½ cup (1 stick) butter or margarine
2 packages (10 ounces each) quick-thaw frozen mixed fruits
2 firm ripe bananas
1 container (4½ ounces) frozen whipped topping, thawed

1 Separate biscuits, following label directions. Place in a single layer in each of two 8-inch round layer-cake pans; press together to fill any holes and make an even layer.
2 Mix flour and brown sugar in a small bowl; cut in butter or margarine until mixture is crumbly. Sprinkle over biscuit layers.
3 Bake in very hot oven (450°) 15 minutes, or until firm and golden. Cool 10 minutes in pans on wire racks. Loosen around edges with a knife; carefully remove from pans.
4 While layers bake, thaw fruits, following label directions. Peel bananas; slice; combine with fruits.
5 Stack biscuit layers, shortcake style, on a serving plate with fruit mixture between and on top. Spoon part of the whipped topping in center. Cut shortcake into wedges; serve with remaining whipped topping.

Apricot-Cake Parfaits
Makes 4 servings

1 package (about 4 ounces) vanilla pudding and pie-filling mix
1 jar (8 ounces) junior apricots
1 cup milk
4 ladyfingers
4 teaspoons apricot preserves
    Whipped cream from a pressurized can

1 Combine pudding mix, junior apricots and milk in a medium-size saucepan; cook, following label directions for pudding. Cool completely.
2 Separate ladyfingers; spread half of each with 1 teaspoon of the apricot preserves; put back together. Stand each in the center of a parfait glass; spoon in cooled pudding. Chill.
3 Just before serving, garnish with whipped cream.

Ginger Peachy Shortcakes
Bake at 350° for 25 minutes. Makes 8 servings

1 package loaf-size yellow cake mix
1 teaspoon ground ginger
    Egg
    Water

A mix-based masterpiece! February Shortcake begins with refrigerated buttermilk biscuits, adds crumbly streusel topping before baking. For the filling— quick-thaw frozen fruits and thinly sliced bananas.

1 package (about 4 ounces) instant vanilla pudding mix
1½ cups milk
1 cup light cream or table cream
½ teaspoon almond extract
6 large peaches, peeled, pitted, sliced and sweetened

1 Combine cake mix with ginger in a medium-size bowl. Prepare with egg and water, following label directions. Pour into a baking pan, 8x8x2.
2 Bake in moderate oven (350°) 25 minutes, or until top springs back when lightly pressed with fingertip. Cool 10 minutes in pan on a wire rack. Loosen around edges with a knife; turn out onto rack; cool.
3 Prepare pudding mix with milk, cream and almond extract, following label directions; chill.
4 When ready to serve, cut cake into 8 pieces; place each on a dessert plate. Spoon peaches over top. Stir pudding mixture until smooth; spoon over peaches.

Checkerboard Peach Cobbler
Peach filling comes conveniently in a can; pastry lattice is simply twists of refrigerated rolls. Bake at 375° for 35 minutes. Makes 6 to 8 servings

1 can (1 pound, 5 ounces) peach pie filling
½ cup firmly packed brown sugar
½ cup seedless raisins
½ teaspoon salt
½ teaspoon almond extract
1 package refrigerated orange Danish rolls with icing

1 Blend pie filling, brown sugar, raisins, salt and almond extract in a medium-size bowl; spoon into a baking pan, 8x8x2.
2 Separate rolls, following label directions; set container of icing aside for Step 3. Unwind each roll into a strip, then twist strip several times to make a rope about 8 inches long. Place 4 of the ropes, spacing evenly, over peach filling in pan; place remainder crosswise over top to make a checkerboard design.
3 Bake in moderate oven (375°) 35 minutes, or until topping is golden. Spread icing thinly over top. Serve warm, with cream, if you wish.

Apple Betty
Bake at 375° for 30 minutes. Makes 8 servings

2 cans (1 pound, 4 ounces each) pie-sliced apples, drained
½ cup firmly packed brown sugar
1 teaspoon ground cinnamon

1219

¾ cup (1½ sticks) butter or margarine, melted
3 envelopes maple and brown sugar flavor
    instant oatmeal (from a 13-ounce package)
2 cups cubed bread (2 slices)

1 Combine apples, brown sugar and cinnamon
in a large bowl; toss lightly to mix.
2 Drizzle melted butter or margarine over oatmeal in a medium-size bowl; toss with a fork
until well blended; measure out ½ cup and set
aside.
3 Add remainder to apple mixture with bread
cubes; toss lightly. Spoon into a baking dish,
8x8x2; sprinkle the ½ cup oatmeal mixture over
top.
4 Bake in moderate oven (375°) 30 minutes,
or until puffed and golden. Spoon into dessert
dishes; serve warm with cream or ice cream,
if you wish.

Apple Crunch
Canned apples, puréed in the blender, then
layered with packaged buttery-rich cookies that
have always rated high.
Bake at 350° for 30 minutes. Makes 6 servings

1 package (10 ounces) shortbread cookies
½ cup firmly packed brown sugar
1 can (1 pound, 4 ounces) pie-sliced apples,
    drained well
2 tablespoons butter or margarine
    Cinnamon-sugar
    Whipped cream from a pressurized can

1 Crush cookies fine. (There should be about
3 cups.) Tip to speed the job: Place cookies,
half at a time, in a plastic bag and crush with
a rolling pin.
2 Place crumbs in a medium-size bowl; stir in
half of the brown sugar.
3 Place apples in an electric-blender container;
cover. Beat until smooth; pour into a medium-size bowl; stir in remaining brown sugar.
4 Press about one third of the crumb mixture
over bottom of a greased baking pan, 8x8x2;
top with half of the apple mixture. Repeat with
another layer each of crumb and apple mixtures; sprinkle remaining crumb mixture over
top. Dot with butter or margarine; sprinkle lightly
with cinnamon-sugar.
5 Bake in moderate oven (350°) 30 minutes,
or until firm and golden. Cool slightly in pan
on a wire rack.
6 Cut cake into 6 serving-size pieces; top with

whipped cream or your favorite custard sauce,
if you wish.

●

Cheddar Pear Cobbler
Bake at 400° for 25 minutes. Makes 6 servings

6 tablespoons sugar
1 tablespoon cornstarch
¼ teaspoon ground nutmeg
1 can (1 pound, 14 ounces) pear halves
1 tablespoon lemon juice
1½ cups buttermilk biscuit mix
½ cup shredded Cheddar cheese
⅓ cup milk
    Light cream or table cream

1 Mix 4 tablespoons of the sugar, cornstarch
and nutmeg in a medium-size saucepan. Drain
syrup from pears into a small bowl; stir into
cornstarch mixture with lemon juice. Cook, stirring constantly, until mixture thickens and boils
1 minute; add pears. Heat very slowly while
mixing topping.
2 Combine biscuit mix, cheese and remaining
2 tablespoons sugar in a medium-size bowl; stir
in milk until mixture is moist, then beat 20
strokes.
3 Spoon pear mixture into a baking pan, 8x8x2;
drop dough by spoonfuls in 12 mounds on top.
4 Bake in hot oven (400°) 25 minutes, or until
topping is golden. Spoon into serving dishes;
serve warm with cream.

Stuffed Pear Crumble
Bake at 350° about 30 minutes. Makes 6 servings

1 can (1 pound, 14 ounces) pear halves
1 can (9 ounces) pineapple tidbits
¾ cup (about 6 slices) zwieback crumbs
6 tablespoons brown sugar
½ teaspoon grated lemon peel
⅛ teaspoon salt
⅛ teaspoon ground nutmeg
2 tablespoons melted butter or margarine
2 packages (3 ounces each) cream cheese
5 tablespoons milk

1 Drain pears; place, cut side up, in baking pan,
8x8x2.
2 Drain pineapple tidbits; save juice for Step
4; stuff pears with pineapple.
3 Blend zwieback crumbs, brown sugar, lemon

peel, salt, nutmeg and melted butter or margarine in small bowl; sprinkle over and around pears.

4 Pour a little pineapple juice over crumbs; cover pan with foil.

5 Bake in moderate oven (350°) 15 minutes; remove foil; continue baking 15 minutes, or until crumb topping is toasty-brown.

6 Mash cream cheese with milk in small bowl; beat until smooth; serve over warm pears.

●

Pear Praline Cobbler
Bake at 375° about 30 minutes. Makes 8 servings

1 can (about 20 ounces) pineapple chunks
1 can (1 pound, 14 ounces) pear halves
½ roll refrigerated oatmeal cookies
¼ cup light brown sugar, firmly packed
1 tablespoon flour
    MINT SPARKLE SAUCE (recipe follows)

1 Drain pineapple chunks and pears separately, saving syrups for making sauce.

2 Split the half-roll of cookie dough lengthwise; slice part into twelve ¼-inch-thick half-moons; press, rounded side up, around sides of a 9-inch pie plate.

3 Toss pineapple with half the brown sugar and all the flour in small bowl; spoon into pie plate, mounding in center; arrange pear halves, narrow end toward center, on top; crumble remaining cookie dough between pear halves; sprinkle pears with remaining brown sugar.

4 Bake in moderate oven (375°) 30 minutes, or until cookies are crisp and brown; serve warm or cold with MINT SPARKLE SAUCE.

●

Mint Sparkle Sauce
Makes about 2½ cups

½ cup sugar
3 tablespoons cornstarch

More dessert mix magic: Party Peach-Bowl Cheesecake (rear), White Mountain Apricot Torte (right) and individual-size Chocolate-Almond Cream Cups.

Syrups from canned pineapple chunks and pears
1 teaspoon lemon rind
2 tablespoons lemon juice

1 Blend sugar and cornstarch in medium-size saucepan; stir in fruit syrups (there should be about 2½ cups).
2 Cook over medium heat, stirring constantly, until mixture thickens slightly and boils 3 minutes; remove from heat; stir in lemon rind and juice; serve warm or cold.

Peach Melba Sponge
Makes 4 servings

1 can (8 ounces) cling-peach slices
 Water
1 package (3 ounces) raspberry-flavor gelatin
 PINEAPPLE SAUCE (recipe follows)

1 Drain syrup from peaches into a 2-cup measure; add water to make 1¾ cups; pour 1 cup into a small saucepan. Dice peaches and set aside.
2 Heat syrup mixture in saucepan to boiling; stir into gelatin in a medium-size bowl until gelatin dissolves; stir in remaining syrup mixture.
3 Place bowl in a pan of ice and water to speed setting. Chill, stirring several times, just until as thick as unbeaten egg white. Keeping bowl over ice, beat vigorously with a rotary beater until mixture doubles in volume and mounds softly; fold in diced peaches. Spoon into a 6-cup mold. Chill several hours, or until firm.
4 Just before serving, loosen dessert around edge with a knife; dip mold *very quickly* in and out of hot water. Cover with a serving plate; turn upside down; gently lift off mold. Serve with PINEAPPLE SAUCE.
 PINEAPPLE SAUCE—Combine 1½ cups pineapple juice and 1 package (about 4 ounces) vanilla instant pudding in a small bowl; beat, following label directions. Let stand several minutes to thicken. Just before serving, stir lightly. Makes 1¾ cups.
Note—Chill any leftover sauce to serve with plain cake or custard another day.

Cranberry Cream
Makes 6 servings

1½ cups bottled cranberry-juice cocktail

1 package (3 ounces) raspberry-flavor gelatin
1 package whipped topping mix
 Milk
 Vanilla

1 Heat ¾ cup of the cranberry-juice cocktail to boiling in a small saucepan; remove from heat. Stir in gelatin until dissolved, then remaining ¾ cup cranberry-juice cocktail; pour into a medium-size bowl.
2 Place bowl in a pan of ice and water to speed setting. Chill, stirring often, just until as thick as unbeaten egg white.
3 While gelatin mixture chills, prepare topping mix with milk and vanilla, following label directions. Measure out about ½ cup and chill for garnishing dessert.
4 Beat thickened gelatin, keeping over ice and water, until foamy and double in volume; fold in remaining whipped topping mixture. Pour into a 4-cup mold. Chill at least 3 hours, or until firm.
5 When ready to serve, run a sharp-tip, thin-blade knife around top of dessert, then dip mold *very quickly* in and out of a pan of hot water.

Easy and impressive: Gelatin-based Cranberry Cream.

Cover with a serving plate; turn upside down; carefully lift off mold. Spoon saved whipped topping mixture in a puff on top.

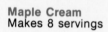

Double Raspberry Parfait
Makes 4 servings

1 package (10 ounces) frozen raspberries in quick-thaw pouch
1 package raspberry flavor self-layering dessert mix
Boiling water

1 Thaw raspberries, following label directions; drain into a 2-cup measure. Add water to raspberry syrup to make 1⅓ cups. Spoon drained raspberries into 4 parfait glasses, dividing evenly and reserving 4 for garnish, if you wish.
2 Prepare dessert mix with boiling water, following label directions, then use syrup mixture prepared in Step 1 in place of cold water. Spoon over raspberries and chill at least 3 hours. Top with reserved raspberries, if you wish.

Pastel and party-perfect: Double Raspberry Parfait.

Maple Cream
Makes 8 servings

1 package (about 4 ounces) vanilla pudding and pie-filling mix
1 envelope unflavored gelatin
1⅓ cups water
½ cup maple-flavor syrup
3 eggs, separated
¼ teaspoon cream of tartar
¼ cup sugar
1 cup cream for whipping

1 Mix pudding mix and gelatin in a medium-size saucepan; stir in ⅓ cup of the water and syrup. Beat in egg yolks; stir in remaining 1 cup water.
2 Cook slowly, stirring constantly, until mixture thickens and starts to boil; pour into a medium-size bowl. Press a small sheet of wax paper on top of pudding. Chill about 1½ hours.
3 While pudding mixture chills, beat egg whites with cream of tartar until foamy-white and double in volume in a medium-size bowl; beat in sugar, 1 tablespoon at a time, until meringue stands in firm peaks. Beat ½ cup of the cream until stiff in a small bowl.
4 Fold meringue, then whipped cream into cooled pudding mixture until no streaks of white remain. Spoon into a 5- or 6-cup serving bowl. Chill several hours, or until firm.
5 Just before serving, beat remaining ½ cup cream until stiff in a small bowl; spoon in center of dessert.

Chocolate Velvet
Makes 6 servings

⅓ cup instant cocoa mix
⅛ teaspoon salt
1½ cups milk
1 envelope unflavored gelatin
3 eggs, separated
½ teaspoon almond extract
¼ cup sugar
½ cup cream for whipping
¼ cup flaked coconut

1 Combine cocoa mix, salt and milk in a medium-size saucepan; sprinkle gelatin over top to soften.
2 Heat slowly, stirring constantly, until gelatin dissolves; remove from heat.
3 Beat egg yolks slightly in a small bowl; slowly stir in about ½ cup of the hot milk mixture, then stir back into remaining mixture in saucepan. Cook, stirring constantly, 5 minutes, or until mixture thickens slightly. Pour into a medium-size bowl; stir in the almond extract.
4 Place bowl in a pan of ice and water to speed setting. Chill, stirring several times, just until as thick as unbeaten egg white.
5 While gelatin mixture chills, beat egg whites until foamy-white and double in volume in a medium-size bowl; beat in sugar, 1 tablespoon at a time, until meringue stands in firm peaks. Fold into thickened gelatin mixture until no streaks of white remain. Spoon into a 4-cup mold. Chill several hours, or until firm.

1223

6 When ready to serve, loosen dessert around edge with a knife; dip mold *very quickly* in and out of hot water. Cover with a serving plate; turn upside down; gently lift off mold.
7 Beat cream until stiff in a small bowl; spoon on top of dessert; sprinkle coconut over cream.

Chocolate-Almond Cream Cups
A twist on a rich-rich French dessert, this recipe calls for two short-cut helpers.
Makes 8 servings

    1 can (about 1 pound) rice pudding
    ½ cup toasted slivered almonds (from a 5-ounce can)
    1 teaspoon vanilla
    1 package chocolate-flavor whipped-dessert mix
      Milk
    ½ cup cream for whipping

1 Combine rice pudding, almonds and vanilla in a medium-size bowl.
2 Prepare whipped-dessert mix with milk and water, following label directions; fold into rice mixture. Spoon into 8 serving dishes or custard cups. Chill at least an hour, or until set.
3 Just before serving, beat cream until stiff in a small bowl; spoon onto desserts. Garnish with more almonds, if you wish.

Coffee Tapioca
Makes 4 servings

    3 tablespoons quick-cooking tapioca
    ⅓ cup sugar
    4 tablespoons instant coffee powder
    ⅛ teaspoon salt
    1 egg, beaten
    2¾ cups milk
    ½ teaspoon vanilla
    ¾ cup thawed frozen whipped topping

1 Mix tapioca, sugar, 3 teaspoons of the instant coffee powder, salt, egg and milk in a medium-size saucepan; let stand for 5 minutes.
2 Heat slowly, stirring constantly, to a rolling boil; remove from heat; cool. Stir in vanilla, then chill.
3 When ready to serve, spoon tapioca mixture, alternately with whipped topping, into 4 parfait glasses; sprinkle remaining 1 teaspoon instant coffee over tops.

1224

Mocha Icebox Roll
Makes 6 servings

    ½ pint cream for whipping
    2 tablespoons cocoa (not a mix)
    2 tablespoons sugar
    1½ teaspoons instant coffee powder
    1 package (8½ ounces) thin chocolate cookies
    1 square unsweetened chocolate, grated

1 Combine cream, cocoa, sugar and coffee in small bowl of electric mixer; whip until mixture mounds softly.
2 Put chocolate cookies together with half the cream mixture in stacks of 4 or 5 cookies. Stand stacks on edge on serving plate to make one long roll. Frost outside with remaining whipped cream. Garnish roll with grated chocolate.
3 Refrigerate several hours. To serve, cut roll diagonally into slices.

Party Peach-Bowl Cheesecake
No one will ever guess how easily you turned out this beauty. Your secret: Cheesecake mix.
Makes 12 servings

    2 packages cheesecake filling mix
    3 cups milk
    2 tablespoons lemon juice
    ¼ cup chopped candied orange peel (from a 4-ounce jar)
    ¼ cup chopped candied citron (from a 4-ounce jar)
    ¼ cup chopped toasted slivered almonds (from a 5-ounce can)
    6 firm ripe peaches

1 Prepare cheesecake filling mix with milk, following label directions. (Save envelopes of graham-cracker–crumb mixture to make pie shells.)
2 Stir lemon juice, orange peel, citron and almonds into prepared filling; spoon into a 6-cup ring mold. Chill until firm.
3 When ready to serve, run a sharp-tip, thin-blade knife around top of large mold to loosen, then dip mold *very quickly* in and out of a pan of hot water. Cover mold with a shallow serving bowl; turn upside down, shaking dessert gently, if needed, to loosen; lift off mold.
4 Peel peaches, halve and pit. Save one half for center garnish, then slice remaining. Arrange part, petal fashion, around bottom of dessert. Spoon about ⅔ of remaining into center, then place the rest, petal fashion, on top. Place saved half, hollow side up, in center.

Unmold cheesecake from tart pan; place upside down on peach half. Sprinkle with chopped candied orange peel, if you wish.

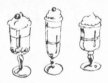

White Mountain Apricot Torte

This layered sweet stars thin pancakes made from a mix, golden jam filling, and quick fluffy frosting.
Bake at 450° for 5 minutes. Makes 8 servings

  2 eggs
1½ cups milk
  3 tablespoons vegetable shortening, melted
  1 cup pancake mix
    GOLDEN APRICOT FILLING (recipe follows)
    SNOW MOUNTAIN FROSTING (recipe follows)

1 Beat eggs with milk and melted shortening in a medium-size bowl; stir in pancake mix, then beat just until smooth.
2 Heat a 7-inch frying pan. Test temperature by sprinkling on a few drops of water; when drops bounce about, temperature is right.
3 Pour batter, about ⅓ cup at a time, into pan, tilting pan to cover bottom completely. Bake 1 to 2 minutes, or until bubbles appear on top and underside is golden; turn; brown other side. Repeat with remaining batter to make 8 pancakes.
4 As pancakes are baked, spread with GOLDEN APRICOT FILLING and stack on an ovenproof plate; spoon SNOW MOUNTAIN FROSTING on top.
5 Bake in very hot oven (450°) 5 minutes, or until peaks of frosting are tipped with gold. Cut in wedges; serve hot.

  GOLDEN APRICOT FILLING—Combine 1 cup apricot preserves (from a 12-ounce jar), 4 tablespoons (½ stick) butter or margarine, and ½ teaspoon rum flavoring or extract in a small saucepan. Heat, stirring constantly, just until butter or margarine melts.

  SNOW MOUNTAIN FROSTING—Prepare 1 package fluffy white frosting mix, following label directions; fold in ¼ cup flaked coconut (from an about-3-ounce can).

Frozen Venetian Parfait

Makes 4 servings

½ cup marshmallow cream
1 tablespoon water
1 pint vanilla ice cream, softened
½ cup ground almonds

2 tablespoons chopped candied red cherries
1 teaspoon grated orange peel

1 Line a 3-cup mixing bowl with foil, allowing an overhang of 1 inch.
2 Combine marshmallow cream with water in a medium-size bowl; stir until well blended; beat in ice cream; stir in almonds, cherries and orange peel. Spoon into lined bowl; cover.
3 Freeze overnight or until firm. To unmold: Invert bowl on serving plate; pull out parfait by foil overhang; peel off foil. Decorate with candied cherry halves, if you wish.

Royal Grape Parfait

This regal-looking dessert goes together fast and freezes into an inviting mauve color.
Makes 6 servings

2 cups cream for whipping
¼ cup sifted 10X (confectioners' powdered) sugar
1 can (6 ounces) frozen concentrated grape juice, thawed
1 teaspoon vanilla

1 Beat cream and 10X sugar until stiff in a medium-size bowl; gradually fold in thawed grape juice and vanilla.
2 Spoon into a 5-cup mold or 2 ice-cube trays; freeze at least 2 hours, or until creamy-firm. Serve in parfait glasses.

Peach Tortoni

Bits of fruit and crunchy cookie crumbs blend with almond cream in this ice-cream–style treat.
Makes 6 servings

  1 package (10 ounces) frozen sliced peaches, thawed and mashed
12 crisp macaroon cookies (from a 10-ounce package), coarsely crushed
  ½ cup cream for whipping
  4 tablespoons 10X (confectioners' powdered) sugar
  ¼ teaspoon almond extract

1 Combine peaches and crushed macaroons.
2 Beat cream with 10X sugar and almond extract until stiff; fold into peach mixture.
3 Spoon into 6 individual foil or double-thick paper baking cups; set on a small tray or cookie

1225

sheet for easy handling. Wrap, label, date and freeze.

4 About ½ hour before serving time, remove from freezer and let stand at room temperature to soften slightly. Serve right in the cups.

Pineapple Alaska

Bake cake at 350° for 40 minutes and meringue at 400° for 4 minutes.
Makes 8 servings

1 package pineapple upside down cake mix
  Butter or margarine
  Egg
  Water
1 square pint cherry-vanilla ice cream
1 package fluffy white frosting mix
  Boiling water

1 Prepare cake mix with butter or margarine, egg and water; bake in a pan, 8x8x2; remove from pan, carefully following label directions. Cool cake completely.

2 Several hours before serving, cut cake in half; place half on a cutting board or ovenproof platter slightly larger than cake. Halve square of ice cream lengthwise; place pieces, end to end, on cake on board, trimming to fit, if needed; press remaining half cake on top. Return to the freezer while preparing frosting meringue.

3 Prepare frosting mix with boiling water, following label directions; spread on side and top of cake, making deep swirls with spatula.

4 Bake in hot oven (400°) 4 minutes, or until lightly golden. Slice with a sharp knife; serve immediately.

Pink Lemonade Squares

Here's a real glamour dessert. Made with frozen lemonade mix, it's unbelievably simple.
Bake at 325° for 15 minutes. Makes 9 servings

1 package (about 7 ounces) vanilla wafers
½ cup (1 stick) butter or margarine, melted
1 can (6 ounces) frozen concentrate for pink lemonade
¾ cup water
48 marshmallows (from a 10-ounce bag or 3 four-ounce packages)
1 cup cream for whipping

1 Crush vanilla wafers fine between sheets of wax paper with rolling pin. (There should be about 2 cups crumbs.)

2 Mix crumbs and melted butter or margarine

in a medium-size bowl; measure out ½ cup and set aside for topping in Step 5. Press remaining evenly in bottom and halfway up sides of a baking dish, 8x8x2. (Crumbs will make a thick layer that bakes into a candylike crust.)

3 Bake in slow oven (325°) 15 minutes; cool completely on wire rack.

4 Combine concentrate for lemonade and water in a medium-size saucepan; heat slowly until lemonade thaws and mixture is hot. Add marshmallows; continue heating, stirring constantly, just until marshmallows melt and mixture is smooth. Chill several hours, or until syrupy-thick.

5 Beat cream until stiff in a medium-size bowl; fold into marshmallow mixture until no streaks of white remain. Spoon into cooled crust; sprinkle saved crumbs over.

6 Freeze several hours, or until firm. Cut into squares; serve plain or top with additional whipped cream, if you wish. Dessert cuts neater if allowed to stand at room temperature about 30 minutes before serving.

PIES AND PASTRIES

Raspberry Mousse Cookie Pie
Makes 6 servings

1 package (16 ounces) frozen raspberries, thawed
1 package (3 ounces) raspberry-flavor gelatin
1 cup hot water
16 marshmallows (¼ pound)
24 lemon-wafer cookies
1 cup cream for whipping
  Brazil-nut curls

1 Drain raspberries; set berries aside for Step 5; combine juice, gelatin and hot water in medium-size saucepan; stir until gelatin dissolves.

2 Add marshmallows; cook over medium heat, stirring often, until marshmallows melt completely; pour into large bowl; chill until mixture is thick and syrupy.

3 While gelatin chills, line bottom and sides of a 9-inch pie plate with cookies.

4 Beat thickened gelatin with rotary beater (this takes lots of beating) or in an electric mixer until it doubles in bulk, turns light pink, and mounds slightly when dropped from a spoon.

5 Fold in raspberries very gently; if mixture gets too soft, chill a few minutes.

6 Beat cream until stiff; fold gently into raspberry mixture; spoon into cookie crust; chill until set; garnish with Brazil-nut curls made by shaving thin slices with vegetable parer from moist nuts.

Pumpkin Tarts

Tiny pies made with custard mix for the smooth richness you like; packaged tart shells for extra ease.
Makes 6 tarts

 1 package (about 3 ounces) egg custard mix
 1 egg yolk
 ¼ cup sugar
 1 can (1 pound) pumpkin
1½ teaspoons pumpkin-pie spice
 1 cup milk
 ¼ cup orange juice
 1 package (6 to a package) graham-cracker tart shells
 Whipped topping from a pressurized can

1 Combine custard mix, egg yolk, sugar, pumpkin, spice, milk and orange juice in a medium-size saucepan. Heat slowly, stirring constantly, to boiling; remove from heat. Cool slightly.
2 Spoon into tart shells. Chill at least 2 hours, or until softly set.
3 Just before serving, garnish each with whipped topping and a canned mandarin-orange segment, if you wish.

Smooth, rich and easy to make: Pumpkin Tarts.

Napoleon Creams

From refrigerated rolls and pudding mix comes a fine facsimile of a great traditional pastry.
Bake at 375° for 13 minutes. Makes 8 pastries

 1 package (about 3 ounces) vanilla pudding and pie filling mix
 2 egg yolks
 1 cup milk
 1 package refrigerated crescent dinner rolls
 1 cup cream for whipping
 1 cup sifted 10X (confectioners' powdered) sugar
 2 tablespoons water
 1 envelope (1 ounce) liquid unsweetened chocolate

1 Place pudding mix in a medium-size saucepan; beat in egg yolks and milk. Cook, following label directions. Pour into a medium-size bowl; chill.
2 While pudding chills, separate crescent-roll dough into 4 rectangles; pinch together at perforations. Place rectangles on a large cookie sheet.
3 Bake in moderate oven (375°) 13 minutes, or until puffed and lightly golden; remove to wire racks; cool completely. Trim edges of rectangles to straighten, then cut each into three 2-inch-wide pieces with a sharp knife; split each piece to make 2 thin layers.
4 Beat cream until stiff in a medium-size bowl; fold into chilled pudding. Spread over 16 of the pastry rectangles; stack in pairs; top each with a plain rectangle. Place on a wire rack set over wax paper.
5 Blend 10X sugar and water until smooth in a small bowl; spoon over rectangles to glaze lightly.
6 Snip a small hole in one corner of envelope of chocolate; slowly drizzle chocolate in parallel lines over glaze. Using a wooden pick, draw across lines to pull chocolate to make tiny squares. Chill desserts until serving time.

1227

CAKES

Orange Walnut Cake
Bake at 350° for 50 minutes. Makes an 8-inch round cake

 1 package yellow cake mix
 2 teaspoons grated orange peel
 ½ cup orange juice
 ¾ cup water
 ½ cup finely chopped walnuts
 ORANGE GLAZE (recipe follows)

Orange-Walnut Cake is as easy to make as stirring orange peel, juice and walnuts into a yellow cake mix.

1228

1 Grease an 8-inch spring-form pan; flour lightly, tapping out any excess.
2 Combine cake mix, orange peel and juice and water in a large bowl; beat, following label directions; stir in walnuts. Pour into prepared pan.
3 Bake in moderate oven (350°) 50 minutes, or until top springs back when lightly pressed with fingertip. Cool in pan on a wire rack 10 minutes. Loosen cake around edge with a knife; release spring and carefully lift off side of pan. Place cake on a wire rack; cool completely. Remove cake from metal base; place on a serving plate.
4 Make ORANGE GLAZE. Spoon over top of cake, letting mixture drizzle down side. Sprinkle thin strips of orange peel over top, if you wish.

ORANGE GLAZE—Blend 1 cup sifted 10X (confectioners' powdered) sugar and 1 tablespoon orange juice until smooth in a small bowl; stir in 1 tablespoon more orange juice, part at a time, until glaze is thin enough to pour from a spoon.

Old-Fashioned Spice Cake

A can of tomato soup is the magic ingredient. Bake at 350° for 30 minutes. Makes an 8-inch double-layer cake

2 cups sifted all-purpose flour
1 teaspoon baking powder
1 teaspoon baking soda
1 teaspoon ground cinnamon
¼ teaspoon ground nutmeg
¼ teaspoon salt
4 tablespoons (½ stick) butter or margarine
1 cup sugar
1 egg
1 can (10¾ ounces) condensed tomato soup
½ cup chopped walnuts
½ cup golden raisins
  LEMON-BUTTER FROSTING *(recipe follows)*

1 Grease two 8x1½-inch round layer-cake pans; flour lightly, tapping out any excess.
2 Sift flour, baking powder, soda, cinnamon, nutmeg and salt onto wax paper.
3 Cream butter or margarine with sugar until fluffy in a large bowl; beat in egg.

4 Beat in flour mixture, half at a time, alternately with tomato soup, beating just until blended. Stir in walnuts and raisins. Pour into prepared pans.
5 Bake in moderate oven (350°) 30 minutes, or until centers spring back when lightly pressed with fingertip: Cool in pans on wire racks 10 minutes. Loosen around edges with a knife; turn out onto racks; cool completely.
6 Fill and frost, layer-cake style, with LEMON-BUTTER FROSTING.

LEMON-BUTTER FROSTING—Cream 4 tablespoons (½ stick) butter or margarine with 1 cup sifted 10X (confectioners' powdered) sugar in a large bowl; stir in 1 tablespoon lemon juice. Beat in 1 cup more 10X sugar, alternately with 2 teaspoons milk, until smooth and easy to spread. Makes about 1¼ cups.

Banana-Lemon Torte

Layer upon layer of mix-made banana cake, with fresh fruit slices and creamy lemon frosting in between.
Bake cake at 350° for 30 to 35 minutes. Makes one 9-inch torte

1 package banana cake mix
  Eggs
  Water
1 package lemon-flavor creamy frosting mix
2 cups cream for whipping
3 medium-size bananas
  Lemon juice

1 Prepare cake mix with eggs and water, bake in 2 greased-and-floured 9x1½-inch layer-cake pans, cool, and remove from pans, following label directions. Split each layer.
2 Blend frosting mix and cream in a medium-size bowl; beat until fluffy-thick.
3 Peel bananas and slice thin; brush with lemon juice so slices stay bright.
4 Place one cake layer on a large serving plate; spread with about ¼ of the frosting mixture; top with ¼ of the banana slices. Repeat stacking with remaining layers, frosting mixture and banana slices, arranging banana slices in a pretty pattern on top. Chill torte about an hour before serving. Cut in wedges with a sharp knife.

Ribbons

Striped with tinted frostings, these three-layer gems look so colorful.
Bake at 325° for 20 minutes. Makes 40 cakes

1 package pound cake mix
  Milk
  Eggs

½ teaspoon almond extract
1 cup vanilla frosting (from a 1-pound, 5-ounce can)
  Red, green and yellow food colorings

1 Line three baking pans, 9x9x2, with wax paper; grease paper.
2 Prepare pound cake mix with milk and eggs, following label directions; divide evenly into prepared pans.
3 Bake in slow oven (325°) 20 minutes, or until a wooden pick inserted in tops comes out clean. Cool in pans on a wire rack 5 minutes; remove from pans; peel off wax paper. Cool completely.
4 Stir almond extract into frosting in a bowl; divide in thirds. Tint one pink, one green and one yellow with food colorings. Spread each on a cake layer; stack layers. Chill. Cut into eighths crosswise, then fifths lengthwise. Trim with frosting rosettes, if you wish.

Ticktacktoe Jewel Cake
Makes 8 servings

1 can (about 1 pound) fruit cocktail
1 package (3 ounces) strawberry-flavor gelatin
1 cup boiling water
1 nine-inch yellow cake layer
2½ cups thawed frozen whipped topping (from a 9-ounce container)

1 Drain syrup from fruit cocktail into a cup.
2 Dissolve gelatin in boiling water in a medium-size bowl; stir in ½ cup of the fruit syrup. Measure ¼ cup of the mixture into a small shallow pan or dish to make a thin layer. Chill until firm for garnish.
3 Chill remaining gelatin mixture 30 minutes, or until as thick as unbeaten egg white; fold in fruit cocktail. Spoon into an 8-inch round layer-cake pan. Chill several hours, or until firm. Place a piece of transparent wrap or foil over a large flat plate. Loosen gelatin layer around edge with a knife; dip pan *very quickly* in and out of hot water; turn out onto wrapped plate. Split cake layer; spread each half with ¼ cup of the whipped topping; place half, spread side down, over gelatin layer. Cover with a serving plate; turn upside down; lift off plate and peel off paper. Place remaining cake layer, spread side down, over gelatin.
Frost side and top of cake with about two thirds of the remaining whipped topping. Press remainder through a pastry bag in ribbons to form blocks on top of cake and rosettes at edge.
Cut the ¼ cup gelatin mixture into tiny cubes; spoon into blocks on cake. Chill until serving time.

1229

Rocky Road Rollup

With a little sleight-of-hand, packaged jelly roll goes homemade fancy in mere minutes.
Bake at 400° for 10 minutes. Makes 6 servings

1 can (about 1 pound, 6 ounces) pineapple pie filling
1 packaged jelly roll
¼ cup semisweet-chocolate pieces

1 Place pineapple pie filling in a sieve set in a bowl; lift and turn filling over and over with a rubber spatula until most of the thick juice has drained off.
2 Unroll jelly roll; spread evenly with the drained fruit to within ½ inch of edges. Reroll carefully; place, seam side down, on a greased cookie sheet. Brush all over with the thickened juice from pie filling.
3 Bake in hot oven (400°) 10 minutes, or until glaze bubbles; remove roll from oven. Dot top at once with semisweet-chocolate pieces.
4 Lift roll onto a serving plate. Slice and serve warm with vanilla ice cream, if you wish.

COOKIES

Walnut Sticks

Bake at 425° for 7 minutes. Makes about 5 dozen

1 package piecrust mix
¼ cup apricot nectar
⅓ cup very finely chopped walnuts
3 tablespoons sugar
¾ teaspoon ground cinnamon

1 Prepare piecrust mix with apricot nectar instead of water, following label directions; divide in half. Roll out, half at a time, on a lightly floured pastry cloth or board to a rectangle about 13x8; trim edges even to make a rectangle, 12x7.
2 Mix walnuts, sugar and cinnamon in a small bowl; sprinkle half over each pastry rectangle; press in firmly with rolling pin. Cut each rectangle lengthwise into 1-inch-wide strips, then crosswise into quarters. Place on ungreased cookie sheets. Reroll trimmings and cut.
3 Bake in hot oven (425°) 7 minutes, or until golden. Remove from cookie sheets to wire racks; cool completely. Store in a tightly covered container.

Butterscotch Chews

Bake at 350° for 30 minutes. Makes 16 squares

1 cup sifted all-purpose flour
1 teaspoon baking powder
¼ teaspoon salt
1 cup firmly packed light brown sugar
4 tablespoons (½ stick) butter or margarine, melted
1 egg, beaten
1 teaspoon vanilla
2 cups cornflakes

1 Sift flour, baking powder and salt into a large bowl. Stir in brown sugar, melted butter or margarine, egg and vanilla until well blended. Stir in 1½ cups of the cornflakes.
2 Spread in a greased baking pan, 8x8x2. Sprinkle remaining ½ cup cornflakes over top; press in firmly.
3 Bake in moderate oven (350°) 30 minutes, or until firm on top. Cool completely in pan on a wire rack. Cut in quarters lengthwise, then crosswise.

Walnut Wafers

Bake at 375° for 7 to 8 minutes. Makes 6 dozen cookies

1 roll (11½ ounces) butterscotch-nut icebox-cookie dough
½ cup granulated sugar
1 cup halved or broken walnuts

1 Cut icebox-cookie dough into ½-inch-thick slices; halve each; shape into balls; roll in sugar; place 1 inch apart on greased cookie sheets; press walnut half in center of each.
2 Bake in moderate oven (375°) 7 to 8 minutes; cool cookies 1 minute, then remove and cool on wire racks.

Praline Crumb Squares

Bake at 350° for 15 minutes. Makes 3 dozen cookies

1 roll (11½ ounces) icebox-cookie dough, any flavor
¼ cup brown sugar, firmly packed

1 Cut off ¼ the roll and crumble into small bowl; mix in brown sugar.
2 Crumble remaining cookie dough into greased square pan, 8x8x2; heat in moderate oven (350°) 5 minutes (dough will melt and cover bottom); sprinkle with brown-sugar-dough mixture.
3 Bake 10 minutes longer, or until top is toasty-brown (do not overbake, as cookies should be chewy); cool in pan on wire rack; cut into small squares.

Caraway Cakes

Bake at 350° for 6 to 7 minutes. Makes 10 dozen small cookies

    1½ cups pancake mix
     ½ cup sugar (for cookie dough)
     1 tablespoon caraway seeds
     1 egg
     ½ cup canned applesauce
     2 tablespoons melted butter or margarine
     ¼ cup sugar (for topping)
     1 teaspoon grated lemon peel

1 Combine pancake mix, ½ cup sugar and caraway seeds in medium-size bowl.
2 Beat egg slightly in small bowl; blend in applesauce and melted butter or margarine; stir into dry ingredients; mix well.
3 Drop by half-teaspoonfuls, 1 inch apart, on greased cookie sheets; sprinkle mixture of ¼ cup sugar and lemon peel on top.
4 Bake in moderate oven (350°) 6 to 7 minutes, or until edges are slightly browned; cool cookies 1 minute, then remove and cool completely on wire racks.

Peanut Drops

Bake at 375° for 6 to 8 minutes. Makes 7 dozen cookies

    2 cups biscuit mix
    1 cup brown sugar, firmly packed
    1 teaspoon ground mace
    ¼ cup soft vegetable shortening
    1 egg
    ⅓ cup milk
    1 cup peanuts, chopped

1 Combine biscuit mix, sugar and mace in medium-size bowl; cut in shortening with pastry blender or 2 knives until mixture is consistency of coarse cornmeal.
2 Blend in egg and milk beaten together; sprinkle peanuts on dough and partly fold in. (If peanuts are very salty, rub between paper towels before chopping.)
3 Drop by teaspoonfuls, 1 inch apart, on greased cookie sheets.
4 Bake in moderate oven (375°) 6 to 8 minutes, or until golden-brown; remove and cool on wire racks.

Spangles

Bake at 350° for 6 to 7 minutes. Makes 10 dozen small cookies

    1½ cups buttermilk-pancake mix
     ½ cup sugar
     ¼ teaspoon ground nutmeg
     ¼ teaspoon ground cinnamon
     1 egg
     ½ cup canned appleberry sauce
     2 tablespoons melted butter or margarine
       Multicolor sprinkles

1 Combine pancake mix, sugar, nutmeg and cinnamon in medium-size bowl.
2 Beat egg slightly in small bowl; blend in appleberry sauce and melted butter or margarine; stir into dry ingredients; mix well.
3 Drop by half teaspoonfuls, 1 inch apart, on greased cookie sheets; decorate tops with multicolor sprinkles.
4 Bake in moderate oven (350°) 6 to 7 minutes, or until edges are slightly browned; cool cookies 1 minute, then remove and cool on wire racks.

Coffee Crisps

Just imagine—piecrust mix and instant coffee make these sparkly-topped wafers.
Bake at 400° for 8 minutes. Makes about 4 dozen

    1 package piecrust mix
    ¾ cup sugar (for cookies)
    2 tablespoons instant coffee powder (for cookies)
    1 teaspoon baking powder
    1 egg
    1 teaspoon vanilla
    1 tablespoon instant coffee powder (for topping)
    1 tablespoon sugar (for topping)

1 Combine piecrust mix, ¾ cup sugar, 2 tablespoons instant coffee powder and baking powder in medium-size bowl; stir in egg and vanilla, mixing well to form a very stiff dough. (If dough seems dry and crumbly, knead a few times until smooth.)
2 Shape into a roll about 9 inches long on wax paper or foil; wrap and chill until very firm.
3 Unwrap roll; slice into thin rounds with sharp knife. Place, 1 inch apart, on ungreased cookie sheets.
4 Mix 1 tablespoon each instant coffee powder and sugar in cup; sprinkle evenly over cookies.
5 Bake in hot oven (400°) 8 minutes, or until very lightly browned around edge. Remove from cookie sheets; cool on wire racks. (To keep cookies crisp, store in a container with a tight-fitting cover.)

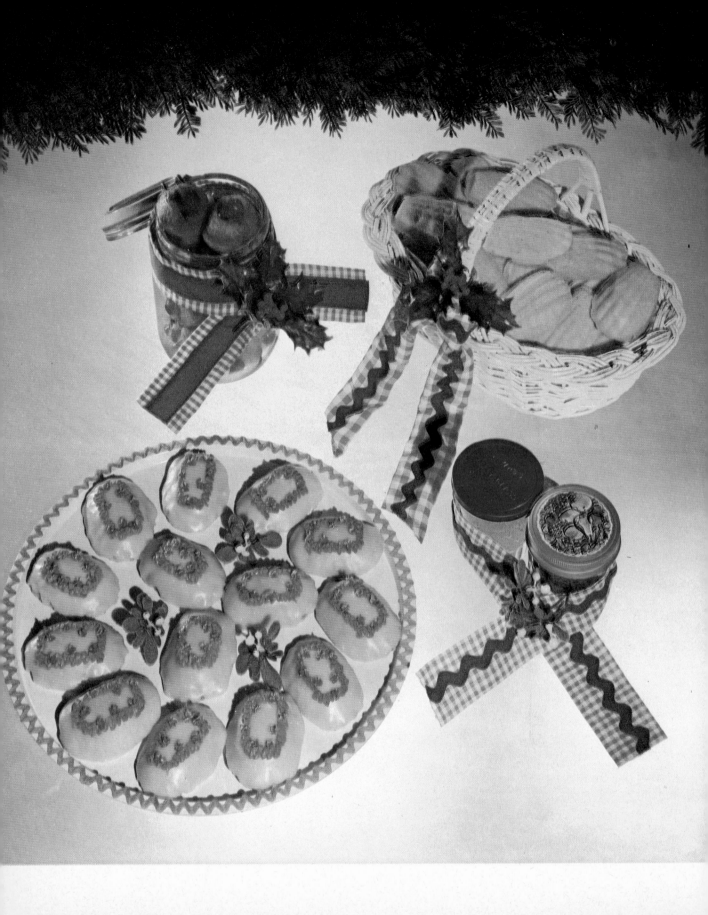

THE JOY OF COOKING

FOR OTHERS

THE JOY OF COOKING FOR OTHERS: RECIPES TO PLEASE FAMILY AND FRIENDS, A PASTA PARTY, A BOUNTIFUL BRIDAL BUFFET, A DAINTY MAY DAY TEA, AN INFORMAL FIRESIDE SUPPER

The true joy of cooking lies in cooking for others. What gifts are more warmly remembered than those baked from a favorite recipe? They contain a special ingredient—LOVE. So, for that matter, do jars of jams, jellies and preserves, boxes of candies, tins of home-spiced or roasted nuts. Anything from the heart and home. It really makes no difference whether the gift is a hearty loaf of bread, plainly wrapped, or a beribboned basket of homemade relishes and preserves. The sharing of oneself is what counts.

For the same reason, the special-occasion party—the birthday celebration, the wedding feast, the club reception—means infinitely more when it is planned, cooked and carried out by the hostess than when it is a catered affair. The fact that the hostess wanted to devote her time and talent to the happiness of someone else injects a special warmth into the party itself.

Even an informal get-together with friends gathered round for nothing more special than the pleasure of one another's company is made all the more warm and welcoming by a home cooked dinner.

Herein lie the cook's real rewards.

A SELECTION OF SERVING STANDOUTS

1233

Holiday Petits Fours
Dainty little cakes, each a picture, with its wreath of Christmas flowers.
Bake at 325° for 25 minutes. Makes 28 tiny cakes

¼ cup (½ stick) butter or margarine, melted
1 package pound-cake mix
2 eggs
Liquid as label directs
½ teaspoon almond extract

The very nicest way to say "Merry Christmas" is by giving a gift from the heart, the hands and the home.

FONDANT FROSTING (recipe follows)
BUTTER CREAM DECORATING FROSTING (recipe follows)

1 Brush 2½-inch oval tart pans well with the melted butter or margarine; sprinkle with flour; tap out any excess.
2 Prepare pound cake mix with eggs and liquid, following label directions; stir in almond extract.
3 Spoon about 1 tablespoon into each prepared pan, filling about ¾ full. (Cover remaining batter and let stand while baking the first batch.)
4 Bake in moderate oven (325°) 25 minutes, or until golden brown and top springs back when pressed with fingertip. Cool 10 minutes in pans on wire racks. Loosen around edges with tip of knife. Turn out onto racks; cool completely. Repeat Steps 3 and 4, washing, buttering and flouring pans between bakings. Wrap in foil or plastic wrap. Freeze up to 3 weeks.
5 When ready to frost, unwrap cakes; thaw, if frozen. Place on wire rack.
6 Spoon frosting over cakes on wire rack to cover cakes completely. Scrape frosting drips back into pan. Let cakes stand about 1 hour, or until frosting is firm. Repeat as in first coat. Let dry.
7 Fill a cake-decorating set with green frosting; fit with leaf tip. Press out leaf garland on top of cakes. Wash and dry cake decorating set. Fill with pink frosting; fit with rosette tip; press out tiny flowers on garlands.
For gift-giving: Place PETITS FOURS on decorated tray. Place tray in gift box (from variety store) without cover. Wrap in wide plastic wrap. Tie with wide ribbon.

Butter Cream Decorating Frosting

¼ cup (½ stick) butter or margarine
2 cups 10X (confectioners' powdered) sugar
1 tablespoon milk
  Red and green food coloring

1 Beat butter or margarine in a medium-size bowl until light and fluffy.
2 Add 10X sugar with milk until creamy-smooth. Divide into 2 small bowls; tint pink and green.

Fondant Frosting

9 cups (2 pounds) sifted 10X (confectioners' powdered) sugar
½ cup light corn syrup
½ cup water
1 teaspoon vanilla
  Green food coloring

Combine sugar, corn syrup, water and vanilla in top of a double boiler. Place over hot, *not*

boiling, water, stirring occasionally until frosting is smooth and pourable; tint green with food coloring.

PIZZA-PAN TRAY *(for Petits Fours)*—Variety-store baking equipment is transformed into a decorative tray—just right for toting goodies. To make, first spray-paint pizza pan glossy white. When dry, glue rickrack to pan edge.

Champagne Jelly
For the ultimate gift from the preserving kettle—tangy, sparkly CHAMPAGNE JELLY. Just the right go-with for the holiday meat platter.
Makes 6 half pints

1 bottle (4/5-pint-size) champagne (1⅔ cups)
1⅓ cups reconstituted frozen tangerine juice
4½ cups sugar
1 bottle (6 ounces) liquid fruit pectin

1 Combine champagne, tangerine juice and sugar in top of a double boiler. Place over boiling water; cook, stirring constantly, until sugar is dissolved. Continue cooking until very hot, about 5 minutes; skim off foam on top.
2 Remove from heat; stir in liquid fruit pectin. Mix well.
3 Ladle jelly into hot sterilized jars or glasses; seal, following manufacturer's directions. Label and date.
For gift-giving: Tie two jars together with checked ribbon ties. Place in tissue-paper–lined gift box (from variety store). Wrap; tie; decorate.

Petits Babas au Rhum
A European confection thought to be named, whimsically, after Ali Baba. Moist and fragrant, a gift for that special friend.
Bake at 425° for 8 to 10 minutes. Makes 4 dozen

½ cup milk
2 tablespoons sugar
⅛ teaspoon salt
½ cup (1 stick) butter or margarine
1 envelope active dry yeast
¼ cup water
2 eggs
2 cups sifted all-purpose flour
3 tablespoons dried currants
  RUM SYRUP (recipe follows)
  Candied red cherries
  Angelica

1 Combine milk, sugar, salt and butter or margarine in a small saucepan. Heat slowly, until butter or margarine melts; cool to lukewarm.

2 Sprinkle yeast into very warm water in a large bowl. ("Very warm water" should feel comfortably warm when dropped on wrist.) Stir until yeast dissolves; stir in milk mixture.

3 Beat in eggs and flour to make a very soft dough. Beat vigorously with a wooden spoon at least 5 minutes, or until dough is very shiny and elastic. Scrape dough down from sides of bowl. Cover with plastic wrap. Let rise in a warm place, away from draft, 45 minutes, or until double in bulk.

4 Beat dough well; stir in currants.

5 Spoon into greased tiny muffin-pan cups, about 1¾ inches across, placing a scant tablespoon in each. (If you do not have enough pans to bake all cakes at once, cover dough and refrigerate while first batch rises and bakes, then stir down before spooning into pans.) Cover; let rise in a warm place, away from draft, 45 minutes, or until almost triple in bulk.

6 Bake in hot oven (425°) 8 to 10 minutes, or until a rich brown. Remove from pans; place, top side down, in a single layer in a jelly-roll pan.

7 Pour warm RUM SYRUP over while Babas are still warm, then keep basting until all syrup is absorbed. Garnish each BABA AU RHUM with a half candied red cherry and slivers of angelica, or green cherries, if you wish.

RUM SYRUP—Combine 1 cup sugar, 2 cups water and 1 jar (12 ounces) apricot preserves in a medium-size saucepan. Heat to boiling, stirring constantly; reduce heat; simmer, uncovered, 5 minutes. Press through a sieve. Cool 15 minutes; stir in ¾ to 1 cup golden rum to taste. Makes 4 cups.

For gift-giving: Fill quart jars with BABAS. Decorate with checked ribbon ties (*directions for making follow*).

Madeleines

Fluted little morsels of lemony sponge cake are equally savored for coffeetime as well as party time.

Bake at 350° for 20 minutes. Makes 4 dozen

  1½ cups (3 sticks) butter or margarine
    3 eggs
    1 cup granulated sugar
    1 teaspoon grated lemon peel
    1 teaspoon vanilla

  1½ cups sifted cake flour
    10X (confectioners' powdered) sugar

1 Clarify butter or margarine by melting over low heat in a small saucepan; remove from heat. Pour into a 2-cup measure; let stand until solids settle to bottom.

2 Measure ¾ cup of the clear liquid only into a 1-cup measure.

3 Brush the madeleine molds well with the remaining clarified butter or margarine; dust with flour; tap out any excess.

4 Beat eggs with sugar and lemon peel in the top of a double boiler; place over simmering water. Beat mixture with an electric mixer at high speed 5 minutes, until thick and light; remove from heat. Pour into a large bowl; stir in vanilla.

5 Fold flour into egg mixture, then fold in the ¾ cup clarified butter or margarine. Spoon into prepared molds, filling each half full. (Cover remaining batter and let stand at room temperature while baking first batch.)

6 Bake in moderate oven (350°) 20 minutes. Cool 5 minutes in mold on wire racks. Loosen around edges with tip of a small knife; turn out onto racks, tapping gently, if needed, to loosen from bottom. Cool completely. Repeat Steps 5 and 6, washing, buttering and flouring molds between bakings, to make 48 MADELEINES in all. Dust lightly with 10X sugar.

For gift-giving: Fill sewing basket with MADELEINES. Wrap basket in clear plastic wrap. Decorate.

SEWING BASKET *(for Madeleines)*—A thoughtful gift for the friend who sews—a pretty basket lined with quilted checked cotton, topped with a rickrack-trimmed tie. To make it, spray-paint a handled small basket glossy white. Allow to dry. For lining, cut paper patterns to fit the basket bottom and side (one long strip), adding on ¾" for seams (⅜" seam). Using paper patterns, cut 2 basket bottoms and 2 side strips of cotton fabric. Place cotton or Dacron batting between 2 fabric bottom pieces and quilt in diamond pattern. Quilt side strips in the same way. Stitch ends of side strip together to form continuous piece. Stitch side strip to bottom, then turn down raw top edge of side strip and whipstitch. Glue lining to basket with white glue.

CHECKED RIBBON TIES—Cut 4"x24" strip of fabric and stitch, leaving ends open. Turn right side out, turn under raw edges and stitch closed. Stitch rickrack down center and tie to basket handle.

1235

Give-aways in gingham dress. Taken from the top, Bourbon Balls, Peanut-Popcorn Clusters, Cherry-Almond Braid, Citrus Peel Glacé and rainbow-layers of chocolate-covered Neapolitan Ribbons.

Neapolitan Ribbons

Bright thin layers of easy-do pound cake sandwiched with tangy apple jelly and lavishly coated with chocolate.

Bake at 350° for 15 minutes. Makes 2 cakes, 2 inches by 9 inches

1 package pound-cake mix
2 eggs
  Liquid as label directs
  Yellow, red and green food coloring
1 jar (10 ounces) apple jelly
4 tablespoons crème de cocoa
2 tablespoons butter or margarine
3 tablespoons light corn syrup
¼ cup water
1 package (6 ounces) semisweet-chocolate pieces
  Chopped pistachio nuts

1 Grease and line three 9x9x2-inch pans with wax paper and then dust with flour, tapping out excess.

2 Prepare pound cake mix with eggs and liquid, following label directions.

3 Measure 1 cupful of batter in a small bowl; tint a bright yellow with a few drops yellow food coloring; pour into one of the prepared pans. Repeat with remaining batter, tinting pink and green with food coloring.

4 Bake layers in moderate oven (350°) 15 minutes, or until cake springs back when lightly pressed with fingertip. Cool in pans for 10 minutes. Loosen layers around edges with sharp knife and turn out layers onto wire racks; peel off wax paper and cool completely.

5 Trim cake layers to square off edges. Cut each layer into 4 even strips, about 2 inches wide.

6 Combine apple jelly and crème de cocoa in a small saucepan. Heat slowly until jelly melts.

7 To make each cake: Place 1 yellow strip on cookie sheet. Brush apple syrup over cake with a pastry brush. Top with a green strip and brush, then with pink strip and brush. Repeat with 3 more strips of cake. Brush sides with syrup.

8 Combine butter or margarine, corn syrup and water in a small saucepan. Heat to boiling. Remove from heat. Stir in chocolate pieces until melted. Beat mixture until stiff enough to spread on cakes (about 3 minutes).

9 Frost cakes with chocolate and sprinkle with chopped pistachio nuts.

For gift-giving: Place cake on decorated picture frame, place frame with cake in gift box (from variety store) without cover. Wrap box, if you wish, in wide plastic wrap, for a see-through effect. Tie with wide ribbon.

PICTURE-FRAME TRAY *(for Neapolitan Ribbons)*—Another variety-store find—an inexpensive picture frame becomes a tiny tray. To make it, take frame elements apart, setting glass aside. Cover cardboard backing with fabric, gluing fabric to back. Insert glass in frame, then fabric-covered cardboard, then plain cardboard for backing. Tape all around to secure.

Cherry-Almond Braid

Tender, sweetly almondy and brimming with nuts and cherries, these coffee cakes make gifts for three.

Bake at 350° for 25 minutes. Makes 3 braids

¾ cup milk
½ cup sugar (for dough)
1 teaspoon salt
½ cup (1 stick) butter or margarine
1 envelope active dry yeast
¼ cup very warm water
4 eggs
5¼ cups sifted all-purpose flour
1 container (8 ounces) candied red cherries, chopped
1 can (8 ounces) almond paste
2 tablespoons sugar (for filling)
1 cup sliced blanched almonds
½ cup 10X (confectioners' powdered) sugar
2 tablespoons water
¼ teaspoon almond extract

1 Combine milk, ½ cup sugar, salt and butter or margarine in a small saucepan. Heat slowly, until butter or margarine melts; cool to lukewarm.

2 Sprinkle yeast into very warm water in a large bowl. ("Very warm water" should feel comfortably warm when dropped on wrist.) Stir until yeast dissolves, then stir in milk mixture and 2 eggs.

3 Beat in 2 cups of flour until smooth; beat in 3 cups more flour to make a soft dough.

4 Turn out onto lightly floured pastry board; knead until smooth and elastic, adding only enough of remaining ¼ cup of the flour to keep dough from sticking.

5 Place in a greased large bowl; turn to coat all over with shortening; cover with a clean towel. Let rise in a warm place, away from draft, 1½ to 2 hours, or until double in bulk.

6 Punch dough down; knead a few times on lightly floured pastry board; return to bowl; cover again; let rise again ½ hour, or until double in bulk.

7 While dough rises, crumble almond paste in

1237

a small bowl; stir in 1 egg and 2 tablespoons remaining sugar until smooth.

8 Divide dough into 3 even pieces. Roll each piece into an 8x10-inch rectangle; spoon ⅓ cup filling in a narrow strip down middle of dough almost to ends. Sprinkle with ⅓ cup cherries.

9 Cut dough on each side from outer edge just to filling in 1½-inch-wide strips with scissors or knife; fold strips, alternating from side to side, across filling at an angle; repeat with remaining 2 pieces of dough. Place on greased cookie sheets; cover.

10 Let rise again in a warm place, away from draft, 40 minutes, or until double in bulk.

11 Beat remaining egg with 2 tablespoons water; brush on braids; sprinkle with sliced almonds.

12 Bake in moderate oven (350°) 25 minutes, or until golden and coffee cake gives a hollow sound when tapped. Remove from cookie sheets to wire racks; cool slightly.

13 Combine 10X sugar, almond extract and 2 tablespoons water in a cup; blend until smooth and easy to pour from a spoon. Drizzle over braids. Garnish with additional red and green candied cherries, if you wish.

For gift-giving: Put each plastic-wrapped braid in a tote or travel bag (*directions for making follow*).

TOTE OR TRAVEL BAG (*for Cherry-Almond Braid*)—Pretty and useful too—plastic-lined drawstring bags can be used for travel or as summer handbags. To make *Pink bag*—Cut 9″x24″ fabric of medium check for bag, 5″x24″ of small check (for trim) and 2½″x17″ of large check (for casing). For trim, turn under lengthwise edges of 5″x24″ strip, pin strip to center of bag and stitch. Stitch rickrack over stitching. With right sides together, stitch side seams of bag with ½″ seams. Stitch casing strip to top of bag with ½″ seam, turning raw ends under ½″ at side seam. Trim all seams; fold casing to outside; turn raw edges under ¼″ and topstitch. Draw ribbon through casing (1 yard pink grosgrain, 1″ wide). For plastic lining, cut 8″x23″ strip of clear plastic, fold crosswise and stitch side seams. (Plastic may be stitched more easily if you stitch through tissue paper, then pull paper away when seam is stitched.) Trim closely. Turn top edges under ¾″ and topstitch. Insert lining in bag.

1238

Bourbon Balls

No baking, no bother, for these deep, dark chocolate confections made merry with a touch of mellow bourbon.

Makes 3 dozen confections

    1 package (6 ounces) semisweet-chocolate
        pieces
    3 tablespoons light corn syrup
    ¼ cup bourbon
    ½ cup sugar
    1¼ cups crushed vanilla wafer cookies (about
        36)
    1 cup finely chopped pecans
    1 container (4 ounces) chocolate decorating
        sprinkles

1 Melt chocolate pieces in top of a double boiler over simmering water; remove from heat. Blend in corn syrup and bourbon; stir in sugar, vanilla wafer cookies and pecans until well combined.

2 Roll mixture, a rounded teaspoonful at a time, into balls between palms of hands. Roll balls in chocolate sprinkles to coat generously, pressing firmly as you roll. Place in a jelly-roll pan; cover; chill several hours.

For gift-giving: Fill clear plastic flowerpots with confections. Put a pink flower in pot (*directions follow*). Place filled pot on clear plastic wrap. Bring wrap up and around pot, with flowers and leaves unwrapped. Tie with pink grosgrain ribbon.

Peanut-Popcorn Clusters

For TV snacking here is a nutty gift for the whole family to munch and crunch.

Makes about 2½ dozen

    ⅓ cup sugar
    3 tablespoons molasses
    3 tablespoons dark corn syrup
    1 teaspoon butter or margarine
    1 teaspoon lemon juice
    4 cups freshly popped corn
    1 can (6½ ounces) cocktail peanuts

1 Combine sugar, molasses, corn syrup, butter or margarine and lemon juice in a large skillet. Heat slowly, stirring constantly, just until sugar dissolves; remove from heat.

2 Stir in popcorn and peanuts; toss until evenly coated. Cook, stirring constantly, over medium heat, 5 minutes, or until mixture is very sticky.

More well made, well meant gifts from the kitchen: (center left) sparkling jars of Lime and Rose Geranium jellies, (rear) Pistachio Mince Crown, (right) Citrus Peel Glacé, (foreground) Spiced Nuts Glacé and (bottom left) celophane-wrapped Lemon Tea Loaf. You'll find recipes for each gift in these pages.

3 Spoon out onto wax paper. Let stand a few minutes until cool enough to handle, then shape into 2-inch clusters. Let stand until coating is firm and dry. Wrap individually in plastic wrap. Store in a loosely covered container.

For gift-giving: Fill clear plastic flowerpots with confections. Put a pink flower in pot *(directions follow)*. Place filled pot on clear plastic wrap. Bring wrap up and around top of pot, leaving flowers and leaves unwrapped. Tie with pink grosgrain ribbon.

CHECK-A-BLOOM FLOWERS *(for Bourbon Balls and Peanut-Popcorn Clusters)*—A gift for a nature lover—new see-through plastic flowerpots blooming with bright fabric flowers. For fabric "rose," cut 9"x12" strip of small-checked fabric and 6"x12" strip of medium-checked fabric for flower center. Starch strips stiffly and iron dry. For flower center, fold strip in half lengthwise and roll loosely to form a rosebud; tack lightly to secure and set aside. For flower, fold strip in half crosswise and seam together. Then fold (so seams are inside) to form a double-thickness circlet. With machine-basting stitch, stitch bottom raw edges together, leaving thread ends long. Gather bottom evenly. Glue flower center to flower with white glue and let dry. For stem, stitch a 14" length of ½" green folded bias tape lengthwise to form casing and insert length of clothes-hanger wire into casing. Attach flower to stem by wrapping green fabric tape securely around flower bottom and stem. Cut green leaves from felt; stitch "veins" on sewing machine. Glue leaves to stem. For "peony," cut 10"x15" strip of medium-checked fabric and 6"x15" strip of small-checked fabric. Stitch each according to directions for flower above, omitting those for flower center. Glue 2 gathered circlets together, one inside the other. Gather a small square of plain pink fabric around a wad of cotton, tack and glue in position for flower center. Finish flower as described above. For an extra-thoughtful gift with the flower pots, you may wish to give a lovely amaryllis or hyacinth bulb to be planted and to burst out in color in spring. You will find bulbs at your local garden supply store.

1240

Lemon Tea Loaf

Sparkly lemon sugar glazes the top of this mellow bread as it cools. Candied fruit slices are a pretty holiday trim.

Bake at 350° for 1 hour and 15 minutes. Makes 1 loaf, 9x5x3

3 cups sifted all-purpose flour

¾ cup granulated sugar (for bread)
3 teaspoons baking powder
1 teaspoon salt
¼ teaspoon baking soda
¼ teaspoon ground nutmeg
½ cup finely chopped walnuts
¼ cup firmly packed brown sugar
1 tablespoon grated lemon peel
1 egg
1¼ cups milk
4 tablespoons (½ stick) butter or margarine, melted
1 tablespoon granulated sugar (for topping)
1 tablespoon lemon juice

1 Sift flour, the ¾ cup granulated sugar, baking powder, salt, soda and nutmeg into a large bowl; stir in walnuts, brown sugar, and lemon peel.
2 Beat egg slightly with milk in a small bowl; stir in melted butter or margarine; pour all at once into flour mixture. Stir about 30 strokes, or just until evenly moist. Spoon into a well-greased loaf pan, 9x5x3; let stand 20 minutes.
3 Bake in moderate oven (350°) 1 hour and 15 minutes, or until a wooden pick inserted in center comes out clean.
4 Cool in pan on a wire rack 5 minutes; turn out onto rack.
5 Mix the 1 tablespoon granulated sugar and lemon juice in a cup; brush over top of loaf several times to glaze. Cool loaf completely; wrap and store at least a day before slicing.
6 Just before serving or giving, trim with CANDIED LEMON SLICES *(directions follow)*, if you wish.

CANDIED LEMON SLICES—Sprinkle 2 tablespoons granulated sugar on a flat plate; place 4 slices lemon in a single layer on top; sprinkle with 2 more tablespoons sugar. Let stand at room temperature, turning two or three times, 2 hours, or until richly glazed. Remove and let dry on wax paper. Decorate center of each with a candied-cherry half.

Lime Jelly

Even if the first snow is on the ground, there's still time to make this tangy sparkler for holiday gifts.

Makes five 8-ounce glasses

1 package (about 2 ounces) powdered fruit pectin
2 cups water
1 cup lime juice
3¾ cups sugar
Green and yellow food colorings

1 Combine pectin, water and lime juice in a kettle.

2 Cook rapidly, stirring constantly, 5 minutes, or until bubbles form around edge of kettle. Stir in sugar; continue cooking, stirring constantly, 2 minutes, or just until sugar dissolves. (Do not let mixture boil.) Remove from heat.
3 Stir in a few drops each green and yellow food colorings to tint lime green; skim.
4 Pour into hot sterilized jelly glasses; top each with a thin layer of melted paraffin. Cool completely; cap; label. Store in a cool, dry place.

Rose-Geranium Jelly
Makes about eight 8-ounce glasses

 4 cups bottled apple juice
½ cup lemon juice
10 cups sugar
 1 bottle liquid fruit pectin
 8 fresh rose-geranium leaves, washed
   Red food coloring

1 Combine apple juice, lemon juice and sugar in large kettle; heat just to boiling, stirring constantly. Stir in liquid fruit pectin all at once; heat to a full rolling boil and boil hard, stirring constantly, 1 minute.
2 Remove from heat; drop in rose-geranium leaves; tint mixture rosy red with food coloring; skim off foam; remove leaves.
3 Ladle jelly into hot sterilized glasses or jars. Label; store in a cool dry place. Jelly takes a week or longer to become firmly set.

Citrus Peel Glacé
Makes about 2 pounds

 3 large oranges
 3 large lemons
 3 limes
 3 cups sugar
⅛ teaspoon salt
 1 tablespoon light corn syrup
1½ cups water
 1 teaspoon unflavored gelatin (from 1 envelope)

1 Cut peels of oranges, lemons and limes in eight sections each, then peel off. Shave off any thick white membrane, then cut peels into ¼-inch-wide strips; place in a heavy large saucepan.
2 Pour in cold water to cover. Heat to boiling; simmer 15 minutes; drain. Repeat cooking with

fresh water and draining two more times. Return peels to saucepan.
3 Stir in 2 cups of the sugar, salt, corn syrup and 1 cup of the water. Cook over very low heat, stirring often from bottom of pan, 40 minutes, or until most of the syrup is absorbed.
4 While peels cook, soften gelatin in remaining ½ cup water in a 1-cup measure; stir into hot peel mixture until gelatin dissolves; remove from heat.
5 Let peels stand in syrup until cool. Lift out strips, one at a time, and roll in remaining 1 cup sugar on wax paper to coat generously. Place in a single layer on a cookie sheet; let stand overnight to dry.
6 Store in a tightly covered container to keep peel moist.

Spiced Nuts Glacé
One bite of these crunchy sweet treats just coaxes you into having another.
Makes about 2 pounds

 3 cups unsalted mixed whole nuts (about 1 pound)
 1 cup granulated sugar
½ cup firmly packed brown sugar
½ teaspoon salt
½ teaspoon ground cinnamon
½ teaspoon ground nutmeg
⅛ teaspoon ground cloves
½ cup light corn syrup
½ cup water
 2 tablespoons butter or margarine

1 Spread nuts in a shallow pan; heat in moderate oven (350°) 10 minutes, or until hot.
2 While nuts heat, combine granulated and brown sugars, salt, spices, corn syrup and water in a medium-size saucepan. Heat, stirring constantly, over low heat until sugars dissolve, then cook, without stirring, to 300° on a candy thermometer. (A teaspoonful of syrup will separate into brittle threads when dropped in cold water.)
3 Stir in nuts and butter or margarine until nuts are evenly coated. Spoon into a well-buttered jelly-roll pan, 15x10x1; spread in an even layer. Cool completely.
4 Break into bite-size pieces, Store in a tightly covered container.

1241

Pistachio Mince Crown
One of the easiest of all fruitcakes to make, this dark moist beauty really needs no extra time for mellowing.

Bake at 300° for 2 hours. Makes one 9-inch round cake

2½ cups sifted all-purpose flour
1 teaspoon baking soda
2 eggs
1 jar (1 pound, 12 ounces) prepared mince-meat
1 can (14 or 15 ounces) sweetened condensed milk
1 jar (8 ounces) chopped candied pineapple
1 jar (8 ounces) chopped candied citron
½ cup coarsely chopped pistachio nuts
½ cup 10X (confectioners' powdered) sugar
1 tablespoon water
Finely chopped pistachio nuts

1 Line bottom and side of a greased 9-inch angel-cake pan with a double thickness of brown paper; grease paper. (Tip: Use bottom of pan as a pattern and cut circles of paper with holes for tube. For side, cut two 4-inch-wide strips long enough to go around pan, then cut slits, 1 inch apart, along one side of each. Fit strips, cut sides down, inside pan. Slits will overlap slightly to make a smooth edge.)
2 Sift flour and soda onto wax paper.
3 Beat eggs slightly in a large bowl; stir in mincemeat, condensed milk, candied pineapple and citron and coarsely chopped pistachio nuts; fold in flour mixture. Spoon into prepared pan.
4 Bake in slow oven (300°) 2 hours, or until firm on top. Cool cake completely in pan on a wire rack.
5 Loosen around edge and tube with a knife; turn out onto rack; peel off paper; turn right side up.
6 To store, place cake in a plastic bag and seal. It will stay fresh in the refrigerator about 8 weeks or in the freezer for 3 months.
7 When ready to serve or give, blend 10X sugar and water until smooth in a cup; drizzle over cake, letting it drip down side. Sprinkle top with additional finely chopped pistachio nuts.

Cheese Log Indienne
Any cheese fan would be delighted to receive this appetizer or dessert fancy.
Makes 16 servings

1 package (8 ounces) cream cheese, softened
1 cup shredded sharp Cheddar cheese (4 ounces)

With each of these gifts, you might include a copy of the recipe (all are included here). Clockwise from top left: Crisscross Cinnamon Square, Hearty Wheat Bread, Spiced Nuts Glacé, Cheese Log Indienne, Lime Jelly and tiny Frosted Cherry Cuplets.

½ cup crumbled blue cheese
1 tablespoon butter or margarine
½ teaspoon curry powder
1 cup flaked coconut (from an about-4-ounce can)

1 Combine cream, Cheddar and blue cheeses in a medium-size bowl; beat until well blended and fluffy. Chill until firm enough to handle.
2 While cheese mixture chills, melt butter or margarine in a small frying pan; stir in curry powder and coconut. Heat very slowly, stirring constantly, several minutes, or just until coconut is lightly toasted; spread on paper toweling to drain.
3 Shape cheese mixture into an 8-inch-long log; roll in coconut mixture to coat well. Wrap tightly in wax paper, foil or transparent wrap; chill again until firm.
4 When ready to serve, unwrap log; place on a serving plate. Frame with bite-size pieces of assorted fresh fruits and your favorite crisp crackers, if you wish.

Crisscross Cinnamon Square and Frosted Cherry Cuplets
One batch of dough makes two different breakfast or coffeetime sweets.
Bake at 375° for 25 minutes for large coffeecake and 15 minutes for tiny rolls. Makes one 9-inch square coffeecake and 4 dozen tiny rolls

½ cup milk
¾ cup sugar
1½ teaspoons salt
6 tablespoons (¾ stick) butter or margarine
2 envelopes active dry yeast
½ cup very warm water
2 eggs, slightly beaten
4½ cups sifted all-purpose flour
½ cup cherry jam (from a 12-ounce jar)
1 teaspoon ground cinnamon
½ cup sifted 10X (confectioners' powdered) sugar
1 tablespoon water

1 Scald milk with ½ cup of the sugar, salt and 4 tablespoons of the butter or margarine in a small saucepan; cool to lukewarm. (Set remaining ¼ cup sugar and 2 tablespoons butter or margarine aside for Step 12.)
2 Sprinkle yeast into very warm water in a large bowl. ("Very warm" water should feel comfortably warm when dropped on wrist.) Stir until yeast dissolves, then stir in cooled milk mixture and beaten eggs.

1243

3 Beat in half of the flour until smooth, then beat in remaining to make a stiff dough.

4 Turn out onto a lightly floured pastry cloth or board; knead until smooth and elastic, adding only enough extra flour to keep dough from sticking.

5 Place in a greased large bowl; turn to coat all over with shortening; cover with a clean towel. Let rise in a warm place, away from draft, 1 hour, or until double in bulk.

6 Punch dough down; knead a few times; divide in half.

7 To shape CRISSCROSS CINNAMON SQUARE: Roll one half of dough to a rectangle, 9x8, on a lightly floured pastry cloth or board; cut into eight 1-inch-wide strips. Place 4 of the strips, about 1 inch apart, in a greased baking pan, 9x9x2. Weave in remaining 4 strips, over and under, to give a lattice effect; cover.

8 To shape FROSTED CHERRY CUPLETS: Roll out remaining half of dough to a 16-inch square; cut into rounds with a floured 2¼-inch cutter; reroll trimmings and cut out to make 48 rounds in all. Press rounds into greased tiny muffin-pan cups.

9 Spoon ½ teaspoonful cherry jam on top of each; cover.

10 Let both doughs rise again in a warm place, away from draft, 1 hour for large coffeecake and 30 minutes for rolls, or until each is double in bulk.

11 Bake small rolls in moderate oven (375°) 15 minutes, or until golden; remove from pans; cool on wire racks.

12 Melt remaining 2 tablespoons butter or margarine in a small frying pan; mix remaining ¼ cup sugar with cinnamon in a cup. Brush melted butter or margarine lightly over raised coffeecake dough; sprinkle with the cinnamon-sugar mixture.

13 Bake in moderate oven (375°) 25 minutes, or until richly browned and coffeecake gives a hollow sound when tapped. Loosen around edges with a knife; turn out onto a clean towel; turn right side up. Cool on a wire rack.

14 Combine 10X sugar with the 1 tablespoon water in a cup; drizzle over cherry rolls.

1244

Hearty Wheat Bread
A plump loaf of this wonderful homemade specialty plus a glass or two of jelly make a thoughtful remembrance.
Bake regular-size loaves at 350° for 1 hour, or large round loaf at 375° for 1 hour. Makes 2 regular-size loaves or one 9-inch round loaf

2 cups milk
¼ cup molasses
3 tablespoons butter or margarine
3 teaspoons salt
2 envelopes active dry yeast
½ cup very warm water
5 cups sifted all-purpose flour
2 cups uncooked granulated whole-wheat cereal

1 Scald milk with molasses, butter or margarine and salt in a small saucepan; cool to lukewarm.

2 Sprinkle yeast into very warm water in a large bowl. ("Very warm" water should feel comfortably warm when dropped on wrist.) Stir until yeast dissolves, then stir in cooled milk mixture.

3 Beat in 2 cups of the flour until smooth; stir in cereal, then beat in just enough of remaining 3 cups flour to make a stiff dough.

4 Turn out onto a lightly floured pastry cloth or board; knead until smooth and elastic, adding only enough extra flour to keep dough from sticking.

5 Place in a greased large bowl, turning to coat all over with shortening; cover with a clean towel. Let rise in a warm place, away from draft, 1 hour, or until double in bulk. Punch dough down; knead a few times.

6 To make 2 regular-size loaves: Divide dough in half; roll out, half at a time, to a rectangle, 18x6; roll up, jelly-roll fashion. Place each, seam side down, in a greased loaf pan, 9x5x3; cover.

7 To make one 9-inch round loaf: Shape dough into a 9-inch round and place in a 9-inch spring-form pan; cover.

8 Let either size rise again in a warm place, away from draft, 30 minutes, or until double in bulk.

9 Bake regular-size loaves in moderate oven (350°) 1 hour, or until richly golden and bread gives a hollow sound when tapped. Bake large round loaf in moderate oven (375°) 1 hour, or until richly browned and bread gives a hollow sound when tapped.

10 Loosen loaves around edges with a knife; turn out onto wire racks. Brush tops lightly with butter or margarine, if you prefer a soft crust. Cool bread completely.

**THREE FRUIT BREADS
TO SHARE WITH FRIENDS**

Mince Loaf
Bake at 350° for 1 hour. Makes 1 loaf, 9x5x3

3 cups sifted all-purpose flour
3½ teaspoons baking powder
½ teaspoon salt
¼ teaspoon baking soda

¾ cup firmly packed brown sugar
1½ cups chopped walnuts
  2 eggs
½ cup milk
⅓ cup vegetable oil
  1 cup prepared mincemeat (from a 1-pound, 12-ounce jar)

1 Grease a loaf pan, 9x5x3.
2 Sift flour, baking powder, salt and soda into a large bowl; stir in brown sugar and walnuts.
3 Beat eggs well in a small bowl; stir in milk, vegetable oil and mincemeat. Add all at once to flour mixture; stir just until evenly moist. Spoon into prepared pan; spread top even.
4 Bake in moderate oven (350°) 1 hour, or until a wooden pick inserted in center comes out clean. Cool in pan on a wire rack 10 minutes. Loosen around edges with a knife; turn out onto rack. Cool completely.
5 Wrap loaf in wax paper, foil or transparent wrap. Store overnight to mellow flavors.

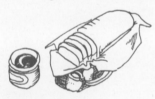

Cinnamon-Prune Bread
Bake at 350° for 1 hour and 5 minutes. Makes 1 loaf, 9x5x3

  1 cup pitted prunes, chopped (from a 12-ounce package)
½ cup boiling water
  3 cups sifted all-purpose flour
4½ teaspoons baking powder
½ teaspoon salt
½ teaspoon ground cinnamon
⅔ cup firmly packed brown sugar
  1 tablespoon grated orange peel
  1 cup chopped pecans
  1 egg
¼ vegetable oil
¾ cup milk

1 Grease a loaf pan, 9x5x3.
2 Combine prunes and boiling water in a small bowl; let stand while preparing batter.
3 Sift flour, baking powder, salt and cinnamon into a large bowl; stir in brown sugar, orange peel and pecans.
4 Beat egg well in a medium-size bowl; stir in vegetable oil, milk and prune mixture. Add all at once to flour mixture; stir just until evenly moist. Spoon into prepared pan; spread top even.
5 Bake in moderate oven (350°) 1 hour and 5 minutes, or until a wooden pick inserted in center comes out clean. Cool in pan on a wire rack 10 minutes. Loosen around edges with a knife; turn out onto rack. Cool completely.
6 Wrap loaf in wax paper, foil or transparent wrap. Store overnight to mellow flavors.

Pineapple-Cherry Bread
Bake at 350° for 1 hour and 15 minutes. Makes 1 loaf, 9x5x3

  3 cups sifted all-purpose flour
  4 teaspoons baking powder
¾ cup sugar
  1 teaspoon salt
  1 cup chopped walnuts
½ cup candied cherries, halved
  1 egg
  1 can (about 9 ounces) crushed pineapple
½ cup milk
¼ cup vegetable oil

1 Grease a loaf pan, 9x5x3.
2 Sift flour, baking powder, sugar and salt into a large bowl; stir in walnuts and cherries.
3 Beat egg well in a medium-size bowl; stir in pineapple and syrup, milk and vegetable oil. Add all at once to flour mixture; stir just until evenly moist. Spoon into prepared pan; spread top even.
4 Bake in moderate oven (350°) 1 hour and 15 minutes, or until a wooden pick inserted in center comes out clean. Cool in pan on a wire rack 10 minutes. Loosen around edges with a knife; turn out onto rack. Cool completely.
5 Wrap loaf in wax paper, foil or transparent wrap. Store overnight to mellow flavors.

1245

FOR THE BIRTHDAY CHILD— PRETTY PARTY FOOD

Carrousel Cake
To show off your merry-go-round, place the serving plate on a footed dish or Lazy Susan. Bake at 325° for 1 hour and 10 minutes. Makes one 10-inch round cake

  4 eggs
2¾ cups sifted cake flour

     4 teaspoons baking powder
     1 teaspoon salt
  1¾ cups sugar
     1 cup cream for whipping
     1 teaspoon vanilla
     1 teaspoon lemon extract
   ⅔ cup milk
     PARTY-PRETTY FROSTING (recipe follows)
  12 animal crackers
     1 long candy stick (about 10 inches)
  12 paper sipper straws
     3 yards colored ribbon, ¼-inch wide

1 Separate eggs, putting whites into a medium-size bowl; yolks into a large bowl.
2 Measure cake flour, baking powder and salt into sifter.
3 Beat egg whites until foamy; add ½ cup sugar (save remaining for Step 5), a tablespoon at a time, beating well after each addition, until meringue forms soft peaks.
4 Beat cream until stiff in medium-size bowl; chill.
5 Beat egg yolks until thick; add remaining 1¼ cups sugar gradually, beating well after each addition until mixture is fluffy; beat in vanilla and lemon extract. Sift in dry ingredients alternately with milk; fold in meringue and whipped cream; pour into greased 10-inch tube pan.
6 Bake in moderate oven (325°) about 1 hour and 10 minutes, or until center springs back when lightly touched with fingertip; cool on wire rack 15 minutes; loosen cake around edge and tube with knife and turn out; cool completely.
7 While cake cools, make frosting. Fill cake decorator with chocolate frosting; using plain tip, outline edges and markings on animal crackers.
8 Frost cooled cake with pink frosting; place on serving plate. Drop mound of frosting (about 1 tablespoonful) onto plate inside center of cake; stand candy stick in frosting; let set.
9 Press sipper straws into frosting, spacing evenly around cake. Place a dab of frosting on center back of each animal cracker; press onto straws, alternating heights; chill cake.
10 Cut ribbon into 6 streamers, each 18 inches long; attach center of each to candy stick with a dot of frosting; drape ribbon over straws directly opposite each other, fastening to straws with frosting.
     PARTY-PRETTY FROSTING—Cream ½ cup (1 stick) butter or margarine until soft in medium-size bowl; gradually blend in 1 pound sifted 10X (confectioners' powdered) sugar and a dash of salt. Beat in 4 tablespoons milk and 1 teaspoon vanilla; continue beating until frosting is thick and creamy-smooth. Measure ½ cup into small bowl; stir in ½ square unsweetened chocolate, melted. Tint remaining frosting a

1246

delicate pink with a few drops of red food coloring. Makes enough chocolate frosting to decorate animal crackers and enough pink frosting for a 10-inch round cake.

●

Jolly Jelly Cake
A triple treat for little tots that's not too sweet and is so easy to eat.
Bake at 350° for 45 minutes. Makes one 8-inch square cake

     1 package (6 ounces) strawberry-flavor gelatin
  1¾ cups sifted cake flour
  2½ teaspoons baking powder
   ½ teaspoon salt
   ½ cup vegetable shortening
     1 cup sugar
     1 egg
     1 teaspoon vanilla
   ¾ cup milk
     2 tablespoons 10X (confectioners' powdered) sugar

1 Prepare gelatin, following label directions, using 3½ cups water; pour into square pan, 8x8x2; chill at least 4 hours, or overnight.
2 Measure flour, baking powder and salt into sifter.
3 Cream shortening with sugar until fluffy in large bowl with spoon or electric mixer; beat in egg and vanilla.
4 Sift in dry ingredients alternately with milk, blending well after each addition; pour into greased baking pan, 8x8x2.
5 Bake in moderate oven (350°) 45 minutes, or until center springs back when lightly touched with fingertip; cool on wire rack 15 minutes; loosen around edges with knife and turn out; cool completely.
6 Split cake horizontally into 2 layers; place bottom layer on cake plate; unmold gelatin on small cookie sheet rinsed with cold water; slide onto cake layer; top with second layer; sprinkle with 10X sugar. Decorate, if you like, with tiny gumdrops or red cinnamon candies, making outline of a favorite storybook character.

●

Ice Cream-and-Cake Rockets
Watch the eyes of junior spacemen sparkle when they see these "fun" treats.
Makes 12 servings

What birthday child wouldn't be thrilled with this mini-carrousel made of a tall chiffon-like cake, encircled with animal crackers riding party straws?

12 ice-cream cones
1 quart chocolate ice cream, slightly softened
1 package yellow cake mix
ROCKET FROSTING (recipe follows)
24 sugar wafers (about half of a 3-ounce package)
Silver candies

1 The day or morning before the party, completely fill ice-cream cones with ice cream; invert on wax-paper-lined cookie sheet; freeze.
2 Prepare and bake cake, following label directions for a 13x9x2 cake; cool on wire rack 5 minutes; remove from pan; cool completely.
3 Cut twelve 2-inch rounds of cake with cookie cutter or use a cardboard pattern. (Use remaining cake for pudding dessert another day.)
4 Frost rounds with ROCKET FROSTING; save remaining frosting for next step.
5 About an hour before serving, quickly put rockets together and decorate: Fill cake decorator with saved frosting; attach medium-size plain tip. For each rocket, place an ice-cream cone upside down on top of frosted cake round. Halve 2 sugar wafers diagonally; pipe ribbon of frosting along uncut edges of wafers and vertical markings on cone. Press wafers into side of cake and cone to make fins. Top tips of fins and cone with dots of frosting; decorate with silver candies, then press more candies into frosting lines on cone. Freeze until serving time.

ROCKET FROSTING—Cream 4 tablespoons (½ stick) butter or margarine until soft in medium-size bowl; gradually blend in 2½ cups sifted 10X (confectioners' powdered) sugar and a dash of salt. Beat in 2 tablespoons milk and ½ teaspoon vanilla; continue beating until frosting is thick and creamy-smooth. Makes enough for 12 rockets.

●

Awful Awfuls
Super-rich thick shakes.

Make drinks, one at a time, this way: Combine 1 cup milk, ¼ cup canned chocolate syrup and a big scoop of vanilla or chocolate ice cream in an electric blender container or electric mixer bowl; beat at high speed 3 minutes. Pour into a tall mug or glass; top with a scoop of ice cream and a generous squeeze of creamy topping from a pressurized can. One quart of ice cream will make 4 AWFUL AWFULS.

For birthday boys (starting at the top) Awful Awfuls, Jolly Jelly Cake with its cinnamon-candy cat, Ice-Cream-and-Cake Rockets (ready for launching—into mouths); for girl guests, Sweetheart Birthday Cakes.

Sweetheart Birthday Cakes
A dainty way to honor a special little girl on her own special day.

Prepare and bake 1 package cherry-flavor cake mix, following label directions for cupcakes (cakes are easy to work with if baked in fluted paper baking cups); cool. Prepare 1 package fluffy white frosting mix, following label directions. Remove paper cups from cupcakes; frost tops and sides of cakes (holding them upside down on a fork); roll sides of each in flaked coconut (you'll need about 1 cup). Top each with a yellow candy rose. Arrange on serving plate; circle with yellow candles in holders (buy them at your favorite variety store). Makes 20 cupcakes.

FOR TEENAGERS— A PASTA PARTY

MENU
Assorted Dips and Dunks
(Use your own favorites or choose from the selection in Appetizers and Hors d'Oeuvres,
VOLUME 1
Crunchy Vegetable Sticks
Chips and Crackers
A-Okay Lasagna
Zigzag Parmesan Loaves
Assorted Soft Drinks

A-Okay Lasagna
It has everything—meat, potato, vegetable and cheese—baked in a golden pizza crust.
Bake at 400° for 45 minutes. Makes 12 servings

Crust
1 package active dry yeast
¾ cup warm water
2 tablespoons vegetable oil
2 cups sifted all-purpose flour
1 teaspoon salt
Filling
2 pounds ground beef
2 cans (about 10 ounces each) pizza sauce
4 medium-size onions, sliced and separated into rings

For birthday teenagers, none of the pastel party bit. The saltier and heartier the better. Lots of chips and dips are in order as are A-Okay Lasagna with its crisscross cheese topping and (crusty) Zigzag Parmesan Loaves.

½ cup (1 stick) butter or margarine
6 medium-size potatoes, pared and sliced thin
(about 2 pounds)
½ cup water
2 teaspoons salt
2 teaspoons mixed Italian herbs
¼ teaspoon pepper
2 cups (1 pound) cottage cheese
1 can (1 pound) cut green beans, drained
2 eggs, slightly beaten
1 package (8 ounces) sliced mozzarella or
pizza cheese, cut into thin strips

1 Make crust: Dissolve yeast in warm water in medium-size bowl; stir in vegetable oil; beat in flour and salt.
2 Turn out onto lightly floured pastry cloth or board; knead 10 times, or until smooth.
3 Place dough in greased medium-size bowl; cover with clean towel; let rise in warm place, away from draft, 30 minutes, or until double in bulk.
4 While dough is rising, make filling: Press ground beef into a large patty in large frying pan; brown 10 minutes; cut into quarters; turn; brown 10 minutes on second side, then break up into chunks; stir in pizza sauce.
5 Sauté onion rings in butter or margarine just until soft in large saucepan; stir in potatoes and water. Mix salt, Italian herbs and pepper in cup; sprinkle half over potatoes. (Save remaining for next step.) Cover; cook 15 minutes, or just until potatoes are tender and water is evaporated.
6 Mix cottage cheese, green beans, eggs and saved seasonings in medium-size bowl.
7 Punch raised dough down; roll out to a large rectangle, 19x15, on lightly floured pastry cloth or board; fit into a greased baking dish, 13x9x2; trim overhang to ½ inch; turn under and flute.
8 Layer half each of potato, cheese and meat mixtures into dish; repeat, ending with meat mixture. Arrange cheese strips to form squares on top.
9 Bake in hot oven (400°) 45 minutes, or until browned and bubbly-hot. Let stand about 10 minutes to set, then cut into squares and lift out with wide spatula. (Casserole may be fixed and baked the morning of the party, then chilled. Remove from refrigerator about 1½ hours before partytime, let stand 30 minutes, then reheat in moderate oven [350°] 1 hour, or until hot in middle.)

1250

Zigzag Parmesan Loaves
You can slice and butter bread ahead, then pop in to heat along with lasagna.
Bake at 350° for 10 minutes. Makes 12 servings

Cut 2 long loaves Italian bread into V-shape slices ½ inch thick, cutting from outside toward middle and through bottom crust. (Keep slices in order.) Melt ½ cup (1 stick) butter or margarine with ½ cup grated Parmesan cheese in small saucepan; brush generously over each slice, then thread onto 2 long skewers to re-form into loaves; wrap in foil. Bake in moderate oven (350°) 10 minutes, or until heated through. Unwrap loaves and serve on skewers.

A BOUNTIFUL BRIDAL BUFFET

MENU
Crab-Shrimp Imperial
Buffet Mousse Ring
Cranberry Crown
Buttered Green and Wax Beans
Buttercup Biscuits
Ripe and Green Olives
Preserved Mixed Fruits
Bridal Cake   Coffee

Crab-Shrimp Imperial
Succulent seafood and rice bake in the richest, creamiest sauce.
Bake at 350° for 45 minutes. Makes 16 servings, ¾ cup each

1½ cups uncooked regular rice
2 vegetable-bouillon cubes
2 cups hot water
2 tablespoons chopped parsley
2 cans (10 ounces each) frozen condensed
cream of shrimp soup
1¼ cups milk
2 teaspoons lemon juice
⅛ teaspoon ground nutmeg
2 packages (about 6 ounces each) frozen,
thawed king crabmeat
1½ pounds fresh or frozen raw shrimps, cooked
and deveined
1 can (6 ounces) sliced mushrooms
1 cup soft bread crumbs (2 slices)
¼ cup toasted slivered almonds (from a 5-
ounce can)
2 tablespoons butter or margarine, melted

1 Cook rice just until tender in large saucepan, following label directions. (Rice should be fluffy-dry.)
2 Dissolve bouillon cubes in hot water in a 2-cup measure; pour over rice. Stir in parsley; set aside for Step 5.

The bride's buffet table should be frilly and feminine, the food should be elegant, the cake one you've made.

3 While rice cooks, combine soup and milk in top of large double boiler; heat, stirring once or twice, over simmering water until well blended and bubbly-hot. Stir in lemon juice and nutmeg; remove from heat.

4 Drain and pick over crabmeat, leaving meat in chunks and carefully removing any bony tissue. Set 2 or 3 chunks, along with 2 or 3 shrimps, aside for garnish in Step 7. Fold remaining crab and shrimps, plus mushrooms and liquid, into sauce.

5 Spoon about ⅓ into a buttered 12-cup baking dish; top with half of the rice. Make another layer of each, using half of remaining crab-shrimp sauce and all of the rice. Spoon remaining sauce over.

6 Toss bread crumbs and almonds with melted butter or margarine in small saucepan; spoon around edge of baking dish.

7 Bake in moderate oven (350°) 45 minutes, or until sauce bubbles around edge and crumbs are golden-brown. Pile saved crabmeat and shrimps in center.

Tips for the hostess: This is a perfect make-ahead to keep chilled or even to freeze. If chilled, take from refrigerator; remove cover, and place in a cold oven; set temperature and bake until bubbly-hot. To freeze: Make in a freezer-to-oven casserole, cool, cover or wrap in foil or transparent wrap and freeze. Take from freezer 2 hours ahead of your party and let start to thaw in the refrigerator, then place in a cold oven and bake until bubbly.

●

Cranberry Crown
It looks so pretty on a party table. The berries literally shine through the shimmering gelatin.
Makes 16 servings, ½ cup each

> 3 packages (3 ounces each) orange-pineap-
>   ple-flavor gelatin
> 2 cups hot water
> 1 can (1 pound) whole-fruit cranberry sauce
> 1 cup bottled cranberry-juice cocktail
> 1 bottle (7 ounces) ginger ale
> 1 cup chopped celery
> ½ cup chopped sweet pickles
> ¼ cup sweet-pickle juice
>   Mayonnaise or salad dressing

1 Dissolve gelatin in hot water in large bowl. Break up cranberry sauce in can with a fork; stir into gelatin mixture with cranberry-juice cocktail and ginger ale. Chill until mixture is as thick as unbeaten egg white.

2 Stir in celery, pickles and juice; spoon into an 8-cup ring mold. Chill several hours, or until firm.

3 To unmold, run a sharp-tip, thin-blade knife

1251

around top of mold, then dip *very quickly* in and out of a pan of hot water. Moisten a small cookie sheet with cold water. (This will keep mold from sticking and make it easy to slide onto serving tray later.) Cover mold with cookie sheet; turn upside down, then gently lift off mold. Chill until serving time.

4 Slide mold from cookie sheet onto serving tray, lifting and pushing mold at the same time with a spatula moistened with water. Fill center of ring with a small dish of mayonnaise or salad dressing; garnish with salad greens, if you wish. *Tips for the hostess:* Make this mold a day or even two ahead, as it will hold well in the refrigerator.

Buffet Mousse Ring

Lots of chicken and ham, tangy pineapple and crisp water chestnuts go into this rich soufflélike salad mold.

Makes 16 servings, ½ cup each

2 *large whole chicken breasts (about 2 pounds)*
2 *cups water*
1 *small onion, sliced*
  Handful of celery tops
1 *teaspoon salt*
1 *bay leaf*
4 *peppercorns*
1 *can (about 9 ounces) pineapple tidbits*
2 *envelopes unflavored gelatin*
1 *tablespoon lemon juice*
3 *drops liquid red pepper seasoning*
1 *cup mayonnaise or salad dressing*
1 *teaspoon prepared mustard*
½ *pound cooked ham*
1 *can (5 ounces) water chestnuts, drained*

1 Combine chicken breasts, water, onion, celery tops, salt, bay leaf and peppercorns in a large saucepan; simmer, covered, 30 minutes, or until chicken is tender.

2 While chicken cooks, drain syrup from pineapple into a 1-cup measure; add water, if needed, to make ½ cup. Stir in gelatin to soften. Set pineapple aside for Steps 8 and 9.

3 Remove chicken from broth; strain broth into a 4-cup measure; add water, if needed, to make 3 cups. Return to same saucepan; stir in softened gelatin.

4 Heat slowly, stirring constantly, until gelatin dissolves; remove from heat. Stir in lemon juice and red pepper seasoning. Measure out ½ cup and set aside for making topping in Step 8. Cool remaining gelatin-mixture in saucepan for Step 6.

5 Slip skin from chicken; remove meat from bones, then dice into small cubes. (There

1252

should be about 1½ cups.) Place in a medium-size bowl.

6 Blend mayonnaise or salad dressing and mustard into gelatin in saucepan. Pour into an ice-cube tray; freeze 20 minutes, or just until firm about 1 inch in from edges.

7 To make the fancy top on mold, set aside enough ham to make twelve 2-inch-long strips, each ¼ inch thick. Otherwise dice all of ham. (There should be about 1½ cups.) Slice water chestnuts very thin. Add chestnuts and diced ham to chicken in bowl.

8 Place an 8-cup ring mold in a bowl or pan partly filled with ice cubes and water to speed chilling. If making a plain top, pour the ½ cup saved gelatin into mold; chill until sticky-firm. To make the fancy top, pour ¼ cup of the saved gelatin into mold; chill until mixture is as thick as unbeaten egg white. Arrange some of the chicken, ham strips, pineapple tidbits and water-chestnut slices in an attractive pattern in gelatin. Spoon remaining ¼ cup gelatin over; chill until sticky-firm.

9 Spoon partly frozen gelatin mixture into a chilled large bowl; beat until thick and fluffy; fold in remaining chicken, ham, pineapple and water chestnuts. Spoon over sticky-firm gelatin layer in mold. Chill several hours, or overnight.

10 To unmold, run a sharp-tip, thin-blade knife around top of mold, then dip *very quickly* in and out of a pan of hot water. Moisten a small cookie sheet with cold water. (This will keep mold from sticking and make it easy to slide onto serving tray later.) Cover mold with cookie sheet; turn upside down, then gently lift off mold. Chill until serving time.

11 Slide mold from cookie sheet onto a flat serving tray, lifting and pushing mold at the same time with a spatula moistened with water. Fill center of ring with salad greens, if you wish. *Tips for the hostess:* Don't hesitate to make this mold a day or even two ahead, as it will hold well in the refrigerator. Unmold about an hour before serving to avoid last-minute fussing. This ring, as well as the CRANBERRY CROWN, should be served on a large flat tray or platter.

Buttercup Biscuits

A quick shaping trick turns refrigerated biscuits into these three-bite dainties.
Bake at 450° for 10 minutes. Makes 26 tiny rolls

2 *packages refrigerated plain or buttermilk biscuits*
3 *tablespoons butter or margarine, melted*

1 Separate the 10 biscuits from each package;

cut each biscuit into quarters; shape each quarter into a small ball.

2 Place each 3 balls into ungreased tiny muffin-pan cups. (You'll have 2 balls left; bake for a cook's nibble.) Brush rolls with melted butter or margarine.

3 Bake in very hot oven (450°) 10 minutes, or until golden. Remove from cups. Serve hot.

Tips for the hostess: Rolls may be made ahead and heated just before serving this way: Place in a paper bag; sprinkle bag *very lightly* with water; fold bag over to close tightly. Heat in moderate oven (350°) 10 minutes.

BRIDAL CAKE

Imagine paying about $5 for this tiered beauty, but that's just about what it will cost if you make it at home. Plan to give two whole days to your loving project, because the cake recipe for the three tiers must be made four times; frosting, twice.

Bridal Cake Layers

Make up this recipe 4 times. Bake 3 of the batches, 1 at a time, in a baking pan, 13x9x2; bake 1 batch in 2 baking pans, each 9x9x2.
Bake at 350° for 40 minutes for large cakes; 30 minutes for smaller cakes

2½ cups sifted cake flour
2½ teaspoons baking powder
  1 teaspoon salt
  ⅔ cup vegetable shortening
1½ cups sugar
  3 eggs
  1 teaspoon vanilla
  ½ teaspoon almond extract
  1 cup milk

1 Grease baking pan, 13x9x2; line bottom with wax paper; grease paper. (Or when baking the 2 square cakes, prepare 2 baking pans, 9x9x2, the same way.)

2 Sift cake flour, baking powder and salt onto wax paper.

3 Cream shortening with sugar until fluffy in a large bowl with spoon or electric mixer at medium speed. Beat in eggs, 1 at a time, beating well after each addition. Beat in vanilla and almond extract.

4 Add sifted dry ingredients, a third at a time, alternately with milk, stirring with a spoon or beating with mixer at low speed, *just* until

blended. Pour into prepared large pan, or 2 smaller pans, dividing evenly.

5 Bake in moderate oven (350°) 40 minutes for large cake, or 30 minutes for smaller ones, or until top springs back when lightly pressed with fingertip.

6 Cool in pan on wire rack 5 minutes; loosen around edges with knife; turn out on wire rack. Peel off wax paper; cool cake completely. Wash, dry and prepare large pan for other bakings.

Bridal Cake Frosting

Make this recipe twice. Use the first batch for Step 4, second batch for Step 8.

1 cup (2 sticks) butter or margarine
2 packages (1 pound each) 10X (confectioners' powdered) sugar, sifted
2 unbeaten egg whites
3 tablespoons light cream or table cream
  Dash of salt
2 teaspoons vanilla
1 teaspoon almond extract

1 Cream butter or margarine until soft in large bowl of electric mixer. Beat in 10X sugar, alternating with egg whites and cream, with mixer at low speed, then beat in salt, vanilla and almond extract.

2 Increase speed to medium and continue beating until frosting is fluffy-smooth.

Here's how to put the
BRIDAL CAKE together:

1 First, make a base for cake this way: Cut a piece of stiff cardboard, 12x10; cover with foil. You will build the three-tier cake and frost and decorate it on this base.

2 Trim cakes this way: You have 3 rectangular cakes, each 13x9x2, and 2 square ones, 9x9x2. Trim crusts from sides and ends of rectangular cakes to make each measure 12x8. Trim square cakes to 8 inches square. If any cake is humped in middle, trim flat.

3 Cut one 12x8 cake in half lengthwise, then cut one half in 2 long strips, each 12x2. *(See diagram).* Cut a 2-inch-wide piece from each end of remaining half and set aside for family nibbles. Cut largest piece in half crosswise to make 2 four-inch squares.

4 Now build the base tier: Place 1 cake, 12x8, on the foil-covered cardboard base. Frost one long side of cut strip, 12x2 (from Step 3); place alongside cake on foil to make first half of base, 12x10. Frost the top all over with a thin coat. Set second rectangular cake, 12x8, on top of base; frost and add second 12x2 piece the same

1253

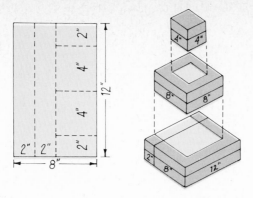

as bottom layer. Frost top and sides with more frosting.

5 Second tier is easy: Use the 2 eight-inch squares. Place the first one flush with back edge of base tier, but evenly spaced on both sides. (This gives a prettier tiered formation in front.) Frost top. Place second cake on top of it; frost all over to base of tier.

6 Use the 2 four-inch squares for top. Center the first on second tier; frost top. Place second square on top of it; frost top, then sides of both squares. *(Diagram shows how easily layers go together.)*

7 Now your cake is completely frosted with the first coat. Set it aside to harden. Frosting makes a thin covering all over cake, and you'll find that the next layer will spread smoothly and easily. Frosting helps to keep cake fresh, so this much can be done two days ahead of reception.

8 One day ahead, make a second batch of BRIDAL CAKE FROSTING. Frost cake all over with a smooth thick layer. Fill a cake-decorating set with frosting. Using fancy tip, pipe an edging around top and bottom of each tier and garlands on sides. Squeeze out remaining frosting to make rosettes on each corner and top.

9 Slide cake, still on its cardboard base, onto serving tray; decorate base with smilax or asparagus ferms.

1254

●

HOW TO CUT YOUR BRIDAL CAKE

You can count on at least 92 servings from both bottom and middle tiers. Usually the top tier is set aside for the bride. She may want to freeze it to enjoy on her first wedding anniversary. The cake will look prettier if the top is left in place until you have cut the 4 sides from the second tier.

Here are step-by-step directions for cutting, following diagram:

1 Start with bottom tier and remove rosettes. Cut a 2-inch-wide strip all the way across the

front. (Front edge of bottom and second tiers will now be even.) Slice strip into 1-inch-wide pieces; place on serving plates. Cut and slice the two sides of bottom tier the same way. (Second tier sets flush with back of cake, so there is nothing to cut here.)

2 Next, cut strips from front, sides and back of second tier the same way, using the top tier as your guide; slice and serve. This will leave another 2-inch-wide band on bottom tier. Slice and serve it next.

3 Remove top tier and set aside. Divide remainder of middle tier in half, then cut each half into 4 pieces. Cut rest of bottom tier in half, then each into 4 pieces the same way.

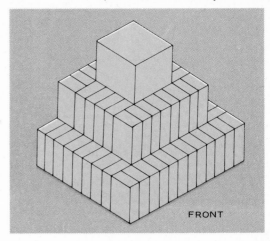

FRONT

JUST BECAUSE IT'S SPRING— A DAINTY MAY DAY TEA

MENU
Sandwich Tray: Strawberry Squares,
Deviled-Egg Triangles, Watercress
Rolls, Lobster
Cups, Ham Rosettes,
Relish Fans
Party Cheese Dome
Muffin Stand: Almond-Cardamom Twists,
Sweetheart Teacakes,
Jewel Creams
Tea
Candied Lemon Rounds
Crystallized Ginger

Strawberry Squares
A rosy half berry tops each bite-size piece of bread spread with tinted cream cheese.
Makes 4 dozen, or about 25 servings

Soften 1 package (3 or 4 ounces) cream cheese in medium-size bowl; blend in ½ cup sliced strawberries (a pint basket will be enough for topping, too), 2 tablespoons 10X (confectioners' powdered) sugar and a dash of salt. Spread 12 slices thin white bread with softened butter or margarine. (It will take about ½ stick.) Then spread with cheese mixture, dividing evenly. Trim off crusts, then cut slices into quarters. Top each with a halved strawberry and a mint leaf. Place on a tray lined with a damp clean towel; cover; chill.

Hostess note: These delicacies keep surprisingly well in the refrigerator, so you can plan to make them on the morning of your party. For 12, make half of this recipe; for serving 100, triple the recipe.

Deviled-Egg Triangles
Peppy egg-salad filling adds a pretty touch of gold to your sandwich tray.
Makes 4 dozen, or about 25 servings

Press 5 shelled hard-cooked eggs through coarse sieve into medium-size bowl. Stir in ⅓ cup mayonnaise, 2 teaspoons prepared mustard, ½ teaspoon salt and ⅛ teaspoon pepper until well blended. Spread 24 slices (about 1½ loaves) whole-wheat bread lightly with softened butter or margarine. (It will take about 1½ sticks.) Spread half with egg mixture; top with remaining slices; trim off crusts. Place on a tray lined with a damp clean towel; cover; chill. At serving time, cut each sandwich diagonally both ways to make 4 small triangles.

Hostess note: Make these sandwiches early on the day of your tea, since the longer they chill, the better they'll cut. For 12, make half of this recipe; for serving 100, triple the recipe.

Watercress Rolls
Flecks of pungent watercress go round and round in these dainty pinwheels.
Makes 4 dozen, or about 25 servings

Wash 2 bunches watercress; snip off leaves and dry thoroughly by shaking in a clean towel. Chop fine. (You will need about 1 cup.) Spread 16 slices (about 1 loaf) very fresh soft white bread with softened butter or margarine. (It will take about 1 stick.) Trim off crusts; sprinkle about a tablespoonful chopped watercress evenly over each slice; roll up, jelly-roll style. (Spread and roll about 4 slices at a time so bread will not dry out.) Place rolls, seam side down and touching one another so they will hold their shape, in a shallow pan lined with a damp clean towel; cover; chill until butter

filling is very firm. To serve, cut each roll into thirds.

Hostess note: Count on about 18 slices to a 1-pound loaf of thin-sliced bread. Be sure it is fresh and soft so it won't crack when rolled. For 12, make half this recipe; for serving 100, triple the recipe.

Ham Rosettes
Delicately spiced ham mousse, cut in fancy shapes, tops slices of crisp toast. Recipe makes lots—perfect for a big tea.
Makes 8 dozen, or about 50 servings

1 envelope unflavored gelatin
¾ cup water
2 cans (4½ ounces each) deviled ham
1 can (10½ ounces) condensed cream of celery soup
¼ cup mayonnaise
2 tablespoons pickle juice
6 brown-'n'-serve club rolls
4 tablespoons (½ stick) butter or margarine
1 bunch watercress

1 Soften gelatin in water in small saucepan; heat, stirring constantly, just until gelatin dissolves. Pour into electric-blender container or into bowl of electric mixer.
2 Add deviled ham, soup, mayonnaise and pickle juice. Beat in blender at high speed 1 minute, or until creamy-smooth, or with mixer at medium speed 3 minutes, or until blended. (If beaten with mixer, tiny flecks of ham will show.)
3 Pour into pan, 13x9x2; chill several hours, or overnight, or until firm.
4 Cut each brown-'n'-serve roll crosswise into 16 thin slices; place in single layer on cookie sheets. Toast in hot oven (400°) 10 minutes, or until crisply golden. (Watch carefully, as some slices may toast faster than others.) Spread with butter or margarine.
5 Cut mousse into tiny flower shapes with a truffle cutter, or into ¾-inch squares with a sharp knife.
6 To put together, top each toast slice with 2 watercress leaves and a mousse cutout. (Butter will hold topping in place on toast.)

Hostess note: Rolls may be sliced and toasted a day ahead, then stored in a container with a tight-fitting cover. Put together about an hour before the party and keep covered and chilled. For serving 100, make recipe twice.

Lobster Cups

Crunchy lobster salad fills hollowed-out cherry tomatoes for this teatime treat.
Makes 5 to 6 dozen, or about 25 servings

1 can (6 ounces) lobster meat, drained, boned
   and chopped fine
1 cup finely diced celery
½ cup finely chopped walnuts
1 teaspoon grated onion
¼ teaspoon salt
2 tablespoons thin French dressing
½ cup mayonnaise
2 pints cherry tomatoes (60 to 70 tomatoes)
10 pitted ripe olives, cut into matchlike strips

1 Combine all ingredients except tomatoes and olives in medium-size bowl; toss lightly to mix; set aside for Step 3.
2 Wash and stem tomatoes; cut a thin slice off bottom; scoop out pulp with the quarter teaspoon of a measuring-spoon set or a demitasse spoon. (Tomatoes will stand flat on stem end.)
3 Stuff each with lobster salad; garnish with crisscross strips of ripe olives; cover; chill.
Hostess note: Have a reserve of these one-bite dainties in the refrigerator, as they'll go fast. For variety, stuff with a favorite ham, chicken or another seafood salad. For serving 100, triple the recipe.

Relish Fans

Slivers of cucumber and radish add a crisp touch to these bread-and-butter sandwiches.
Makes 4 dozen, or about 25 servings

Spread 12 thin slices white bread with softened butter or margarine. (It will take about ¾ stick.) Cut a round out of each slice with a 3- or 3½-inch cutter, then cut in quarters to make 4 wedges. Place in single layer on a tray lined with a damp clean towel; cover lightly while fixing vegetables. Score 1 small cucumber; slice thin, then cut each slice into quarters. Wash and trim 1 bunch (about 12) small radishes; slice very thin. Arrange 2 or 3 radish slices, overlapping, on each wedge of buttered bread; top with a wedge of cucumber. Cover; chill.
Hostess note: Vegetable toppings can be put on about 2 hours ahead if tray is covered and kept chilled. For 12, make half of this recipe; for serving 100, triple the recipe.

Party Cheese Dome

It will be the talk of your tea, as stacked beneath the pale-pink cheese frosting are sandwiches of homemade orange bread.
Bake at 350° for 1 hour. Makes 4 dozen, or about 25 servings

3 large seedless oranges
1 cup water
1 cup granulated sugar
½ cup firmly packed brown sugar
2 tablespoons butter or margarine
3 cups sifted all-purpose flour
3 teaspoons baking powder
1 teaspoon salt
1 egg
1 cup milk
1 jar (5 ounces) pineapple-cheese spread
   PARTY CHEESE TOPPING (recipe follows)

1 Pare peel *very thin* from oranges with vegetable parer or sharp knife; cut into matchlike strips. Simmer in water in medium-size saucepan 30 minutes, or until soft; drain.
2 Stir in granulated and brown sugars and butter or margarine. Heat, stirring constantly, 5 minutes, or until butter melts and sugars dissolve; cool slightly.
3 Sift flour, baking powder and salt into medium-size bowl. Beat egg in 4-cup measure; stir in milk and orange-sugar mixture; stir into dry ingredients just until blended. Pour into greased ovenproof 8-cup bowl.
4 Bake in moderate oven (350°) 1 hour, or until firm and wooden pick inserted in center comes out clean. Cool 5 minutes; turn out onto wire rack; cool completely. Wrap in wax paper, foil or transparent wrap; store overnight, since a day-old loaf slices better.
5 To make sandwich loaf: Trim large end slightly, if needed, so loaf will lie flat. Cut loaf crosswise into 12 thin even slices with very sharp long-blade knife. Put each two slices together with pineapple-cheese spread to make 6 round sandwiches of graduating sizes. Stack back together in bowl shape; place on small cookie sheet or large plate. Frost with PARTY CHEESE TOPPING; chill.
6 Cut loaf into 8 wedges; transfer to serving plate with wide spatula, setting back into shape; garnish with a maraschino cherry with stem on, if you like. To serve, separate one wedge at a time into its 6 tea-size sandwiches; arrange around loaf.

The prettiest of all tea tables is the one showing a contrast of shapes, colors, textures and flavors. This one fills the bill. You'll find all of the recipes for sandwiches, canapes and cakes in A Dainty May Day Tea.

PARTY CHEESE TOPPING—Blend 6 ounces cream cheese (from an 8-ounce package), ½ cup 10X (confectioners' powdered) sugar and 1 tablespoon lemon juice until smooth in small bowl. Blend in a few drops red food coloring to tint a delicate pink. Makes enough to frost one 8-cup-bowl loaf.

Hostess note: For a large tea, you couldn't choose a showier, better-tasting sandwich. Loaves can be baked 2 or 3 days ahead, wrapped and stored, ready to be made into sandwiches and frosted the day of your party. For serving 100, bake 3 loaves.

Almond-Cardamom Twists

Sweet almond-rich filling peeks through each spiral of golden-crisp pastry.
Bake at 375° for 20 minutes. Makes 4 dozen, or about 25 servings

½ cup blanched almonds
1 egg
1 tablespoon water
¼ cup sugar
2 cups sifted all-purpose flour
1 teaspoon salt
¼ teaspoon ground cardamom
⅔ cup vegetable shortening
4 to 5 tablespoons water

1 Put almonds through food chopper, using fine blade, or chop fine in an electric blender.
2 Beat egg in small bowl; measure 1 tablespoonful into a custard cup; stir in 1 tablespoon water. (Save for brushing twists in Step 5.) Stir almonds and sugar into egg in bowl. (Save for Step 4.)
3 Sift flour, salt and cardamom into medium-size bowl; cut in shortening with pastry blender until mixture is crumbly. Stir in 4 to 5 tablespoons water with a fork just until dough holds together.
4 Roll out, half at a time, to rectangle, 12x8, on lightly floured pastry cloth or board; cut in half lengthwise. Spread one half evenly with half of filling, then top with other half of dough; press layers together lightly with rolling pin; trim edges, if needed. Rectangle should measure 12x4.
5 Cut crosswise into 24 ½-inch-wide strips with sharp knife. Carefully twist each strip; place, 1 inch apart, on greased cookie sheet. Repeat with remaining dough and filling to make 48 twists. Brush saved egg mixture lightly over twists.
6 Bake in moderate oven (375°) 20 minutes,

1258

or until golden. Remove at once to wire racks with spatula; let cool completely.
Hostess note: For a large party, make up twists but do not bake, then freeze or store in refrigerator. On party day, bake as in Step 6, allowing a few extra minutes if twists are frozen. For serving 100, make the recipe three times.

Sweetheart Teacakes

Just two bites—and these jam-filled dainties are gone!
Bake at 350° for 20 minutes. Makes 4 dozen, or about 25 servings

1 package yellow-cake mix
1 package (about 7 ounces) vanilla-flavor creamy frosting mix
1 cup apricot jam
Red Cinnamon heart-shape candies

1 Grease jelly-roll pan, 15x10x1; line with wax paper; grease paper.
2 Prepare cake mix, following label directions; spread batter evenly into prepared pan.
3 Bake in moderate oven (350°) 20 minutes, or until center springs back when lightly pressed with fingertip. Cool slightly on wire rack; remove from pan; peel off paper; cool completely.
4 Set cake flat on cutting board or counter top; cut out 48 tiny rounds with a 1½-inch cutter. Split each round and put together with jam. (Use cake trimmings for family nibbles.)
5 Prepare frosting mix, following label directions; spread on tops of cakes; decorate each with a cinnamon candy.
Hostess note: Planning a big party? Add a bonus dozen cakes by cutting layer this way: Trim crusts from cake; cut cake crosswise into 10 narrow strips, then lengthwise into 6 strips to make 60 small cakes. Split, fill and frost the same as rounds. For serving 100, bake 2 cakes.

Candied Lemon Rounds

Each glistening slice adds sweetness as well as tang to a cup of tea.
Makes about 25 servings

Slice 3 large lemons very thin. (You should get about 10 slices from each.) Sprinkle ½ cup sugar over bottom of large platter; arrange lemon slices in a single layer over sugar; sprinkle with an additional ½ cup sugar. Let stand at room temperature, turning 2 or 3 times, 2 hours, or until slices are glazed. Remove and lay between sheets of wax paper or foil until serving time.

Jewel Creams

They look like miniature French pastries—taste like rich, rich cheesecake.
Bake at 375° for 10 minutes. Makes 4 dozen, or about 25 servings

Crust

  4 tablespoons (½ stick) butter or margarine
  ⅓ cup sugar
  1 egg
  ¼ teaspoon vanilla
  1 cup sifted all-purpose flour
  ¼ teaspoon salt

Filling

  ½ cup sugar
  1 envelope unflavored gelatin
  2 eggs, separated
  1 cup milk
  2 packages (8 ounces each) cream cheese, softened
  3 tablespoons lemon juice
1½ cups cream for whipping

Frosting

  1 cup 10X (confectioners' powdered) sugar
  4 tablespoons (½ stick) butter or margarine
  1 tablespoon milk
  ½ teaspoon vanilla
  ½ teaspoon lemon extract
  2 drops yellow food coloring
    Silver candies

1 Mark off a rectangle, 12x8, on each of 2 cookie sheets; grease. (If you have only 1 cookie sheet, bake half of batter at a time.)
2 Make crust: Cream butter or margarine with sugar until fluffy in small bowl; beat in egg and vanilla; gradually sift in flour and salt, blending well to make a very soft cookielike batter.
3 Spread half evenly and thinly into each rectangle as marked on cookie sheets.
4 Bake in moderate oven (375°) 10 minutes, or until golden. Cool slightly on cookie sheets on wire racks, then remove each layer very carefully with long spatula. Cool completely on wire racks. (Layers are very thin and fragile. If one should break, it won't show when put together with filling.)
5 Make filling: Combine ¼ cup sugar and gelatin in top of double boiler. (Save remaining ¼ cup sugar for Step 8.) Beat egg yolks slightly with a fork in a small bowl; stir in milk, then strain into gelatin mixture.
6 Heat over simmering water, stirring constantly, 10 minutes, or until gelatin dissolves and mixture coats a metal spoon; remove from heat.
7 Slice and blend in cream cheese, then lemon juice, until completely smooth. Chill 15 minutes,

or just until thick enough to mound slightly on a spoon.
8 Beat egg whites until foamy-white and double in volume in large bowl; beat in saved ¼ cup sugar, 1 tablespoon at a time, until meringue forms soft peaks. Beat cream until stiff in medium-size bowl.
9 Beat thickened gelatin mixture until fluffy-light; gently fold into meringue, then fold in cream until no streaks of white remain.
10 Place one crust in bottom of baking pan, 13x9x2; spoon filling over crust, spreading evenly. Top with second crust; chill overnight.
11 Make frosting: Blend 10X sugar with butter or margarine, milk, vanilla and lemon extract in small bowl, then beat until thick and smooth. Blend in food coloring to tint pale yellow.
12 Cut cheesecake crosswise into 8 even strips, then lengthwise into 6 strips to make 48 small cakes. Remove from pan; place on cookie sheet.
13 Fill cake decorator with frosting; make a flower on top of each cake; decorate with a silver candy. Keep chilled until serving time.
Hostess note: When cake is served directly from refrigerator, it is firm enough to eat finger style. If it must stand on the table for a while, you may like to provide small plates and forks. For serving 100, make 3 cakes.

HOW TO MAKE TEA IN QUANTITY

For a party of 12, make tea as you do for the family, allowing 1 teaspoon, or 1 tea bag, for each cup. Heat pot first by filling with boiling water; empty; measure in tea; pour freshly boiling water over (¾ measuring cup for each 1 teaspoon tea); cover; brew 3 to 5 minutes. Have a second pot of hot water handy for those who prefer a weaker brew.

For serving a larger group, it's easier to start with TEA ESSENCE. To make: Measure 1 cup loose tea, or 30 tea bags, into a heated 6-cup pot; pour over 4 cups freshly boiling water. Cover; brew 5 minutes, then strain. It is now ready to serve in either of these ways: (1) Pour about 1 tablespoonful from serving pot into a cup and fill cup with hot water from a second pot. (2) Measure ½ cup TEA ESSENCE at a time into a heated 6-cup serving pot; fill with freshly boiling water; pour directly into cups. Recipe makes about 50 cups, or enough for 25 guests.
Hostess note: Instant tea makes a delicious quick brew also. Measure 1 level teaspoonful

1259

for each cup into teapot; fill with boiling water. Plan on 2 cups of tea for each guest when entertaining a group of 25 or fewer, 1½ cups for a larger group.

A Tea Shopping List

	25 guests*	100 guests
Tea, loose	3 ounces	¾ pound
bags	25	8 dozen
instant	¾-ounce jar	4 jars
Cube sugar	8 ounces	2 pounds
Cream	1½ cups	6 cups
Crystallized		
ginger	4 ounces	1 pound
Lemons	3	1 dozen

*For 12 guests, you will need about half these amounts.

FOR BEST OF FRIENDS— AN INFORMAL FIRESIDE SUPPER

MENU
Hot Cinnamon Sparkle
Parmesan Crisps
Chicken à l'Orange
Chive Risotto   Casserole Peas
Lotus Salad Bowl
Macaroon Custard Tarts
Coffee

Hot Cinnamon Sparkle
Makes 8 servings

1 can (46 ounces) unsweetened pineapple juice
1 container (3¼ ounces) red cinnamon candies
½ cup bottled grenadine syrup
¼ cup lemon juice

1 Combine pineapple juice, cinnamon candies and grenadine syrup in a medium-size saucepan.
2 Heat, stirring, until candies melt and mixture is hot; stir in lemon juice. Pour into mugs; serve warm.

●

Parmesan Crisps
Bake at 425° for 8 minutes. Makes about 8 dozen

1 package piecrust mix
1 envelope Parmesan salad dressing mix
5 tablespoons cold water

1260

1 Combine piecrust mix and dry salad dressing mix in a large bowl. Sprinkle water over top, 1 tablespoon at a time; mix lightly with a fork.
2 Roll out, half at a time, ⅛ inch thick, on a lightly floured pastry cloth or board; cut into 1½-inch rounds with a plain or fluted cutter. Place on a large cookie sheet.
3 Bake in hot oven (425°) 8 minutes, or until golden. Serve warm or cold.

Chicken à l'Orange
Bake at 350° for 1 hour. Makes 8 servings

8 boneless chicken breasts, weighing about 10 ounces each
⅓ cup sifted all-purpose flour
1½ teaspoons salt
1 teaspoon garlic powder
½ teaspoon paprika
⅓ cup sliced almonds
5 tablespoons butter or margarine
1 can (6 ounces) frozen concentrated orange juice
1½ cups water
1 teaspoon leaf rosemary, crumbled
¼ teaspoon leaf thyme, crumbled
2 tablespoons cornstarch
CHIVE RISOTTO (recipe follows)

1 Coat chicken with a mixture of flour, 1 teaspoon salt, garlic powder and paprika.
2 Sauté almonds in butter or margarine until golden in a large frying pan; remove from pan. Brown chicken breasts in drippings in same pan; place in a single layer in a baking pan, 13x9x2. Pour all drippings from pan.
3 Stir orange-juice concentrate, water, rosemary, thyme and ½ teaspoon salt into pan. Heat to boiling; pour over chicken; cover.
4 Bake in moderate oven (350°) 1 hour, or until chicken is tender. Remove to another pan; keep warm. Reheat liquid in baking pan to boiling; thicken with cornstarch.
5 Spoon CHIVE RISOTTO onto a large serving platter; arrange chicken over rice; sprinkle with almonds. Serve sauce separately to spoon over chicken.
CHIVE RISOTTO—Sauté 2½ cups packaged enriched precooked rice in 3 tablespoons butter or margarine, stirring constantly, until golden in a large frying pan. Drain liquid from 2 cans (3 or 4 ounces each) chopped mushrooms into a 4-cup measure; add water to make 2½ cups. Stir into rice with mushrooms, 3 envelopes instant chicken broth, and ¼ cup cut chives. Heat to boiling; cover; remove from heat. Let stand 10 minutes. Makes 8 servings.

Is anything more warming on a frosty-cold day than a group of old friends sharing an Informal Fireside Supper?

Casserole Peas

Bake at 350° for 25 minutes. Makes 8 servings

    3 packages (8 ounces each) frozen green
        peas with cream sauce
    3 tablespoons butter or margarine
 2¼ cups milk
    1 cup crunchy nutlike cereal nuggets
    1 package (4 ounces) shredded Cheddar
        cheese

1 Prepare peas with butter or margarine and milk, following label directions. Mix cereal and cheese in a bowl; set aside ½ cup.
2 Layer one third of the peas into a 7-cup baking dish; sprinkle with half of the remaining cereal mixture. Repeat layers. Spoon remaining peas on top; sprinkle with the ½ cup cereal mixture.
3 Bake in moderate oven (350°) 25 minutes, or until bubbly and topping is lightly toasted.

●

Lotus Salad Bowl

Makes 8 servings

    1 envelope blue cheese salad dressing mix
    1 teaspoon sugar
  ¼ cup lemon juice
    2 tablespoons water
  ⅔ cup vegetable oil
    1 large head romaine
    1 bunch watercress
    2 packages (10 ounces each) frozen peaches,
        thawed and drained
    2 cups seedless green grapes
    1 can (5 ounces) water chestnuts, sliced

1 Combine dressing mix, sugar, lemon juice and water in a jar with a tight lid; shake well. Add vegetable oil; shake again. Set aside.

2 Line a large salad bowl with romaine leaves; break remainder in bite-size pieces and place in bottom. Pull leaves from watercress; discard stems.
3 Arrange watercress, peach slices and grapes in rings around edge in bowl; overlap water chestnuts in center.
4 Pour about ½ cup salad dressing over all; toss lightly. Serve with additional dressing.

●

Macaroon Custard Tarts

Bake shells at 425° for 15 minutes. Makes 6 servings

  ½ package piecrust mix
    1 package (3 ounces) egg-custard mix
 1⅓ cups milk
    1 cup thawed frozen whipped topping
  ½ cup macaroon crumbs
        Mandarin-orange segments, well drained

1 Prepare piecrust mix, following label directions, or make pastry from your favorite single-crust recipe. Roll out, ⅛ inch thick, on a lightly floured pastry cloth or board. Cut into 4½-inch rounds; fit each into a 3-inch tart-shell pan. Prick shells well all over with a fork. Set pans in a jelly-roll pan for easy handling.
2 Bake in hot oven (425°) 15 minutes, or until golden. Cool completely in pans on a wire rack.
3 Prepare custard mix with the 1⅓ cups milk, following label directions; pour into a medium-size bowl. Set bowl in a pan of ice and water to speed cooling. Chill, stirring several times, until completely cold; fold in whipped topping and macaroon crumbs. Spoon into tart shells.
4 Chill several hours, or until firm. Just before serving, garnish each tart with a rosette of mandarin-orange segments.

1261

LAND OF PLENTY

LAND OF PLENTY PRESERVES: CANNY WAYS TO SPEED UP CANNING, TOMATOES AND TOMATO SAUCES, MARMALADES AND PRESERVES, PICKLES, RELISHES AND CHUTNEYS

Women who haven't canned in years are bringing down the big kettles. And women who have never canned are trying their hands. There's a delicious nostalgia about the arts of canning, pickling and preserving, a total involvement with food that brings special rewards.

Moreover, preserving food today is prompted more by love than necessity. There's no longer that tedious job of peeling, coring and slicing mountains of fruit, all in a frantic rush to get them into jars before they spoil. And there's no longer the back-breaking job of picking fruit. Today it's simply picked *out* at the local supermarket or roadside stand. So, what was once a monumental chore, a drudgery everyone dreaded from harvest season to the next, has become fun.

The Methods of Processing:

The Hot-Water-Bath Canner: This method is recommended for tomatoes and fruits. These are acid foods and may be canned safely at boiling temperatures. A water-bath canner is simply a large kettle or pail that is deep enough to cover jars at least 1 inch over the tops, with a little extra space for boiling. It must have a rack to hold jars at least ½ inch above the bottom of the canner. It should have a cover to keep the water at a rolling boil during the processing. Both jars and lids should be thoroughly washed in hot soapy water and then rinsed before starting.

The Pressure Canner: The steam-pressure canner is recommended for all other vegetables, meats, poultry and other low-acid foods. This canner is a heavy kettle with a cover that can be clamped down to make it steamtight. The cover is fitted with a safety valve, vent and a pressure gauge. Simply follow the manufacturer's instructions when using.

The Open Kettle: This method is recommended for jams, jellies, preserves, relishes and some pickles. In this method, the food is cooked in an uncovered kettle and poured boiling hot into sterilized hot jars. You may use either jelly glasses or half-pint jars. The jelly glasses need hot paraffin for sealing; the jars require the two-piece tops.

About Jars and Closures: Canning jars are available in half-pint, pint, pint-and-a-half, quart and half-gallon sizes. The most popular lids for

1263

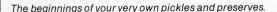
The beginnings of your very own pickles and preserves.

sealing are the two-piece metal ones that form a vacuum on cooling to keep the jars airtight. You can hear the "ping" from the forming vacuum when the domed lids are snapped down. Jars and lids must be pristinely clean before being used.

The best jars for jams, jellies and preserves are either the half-pint canning jars with the two-piece tops of plain or decorative jelly glasses that must be sealed with melted paraffin.

How to Sterilize Jars and Closures: Wash well in hot soapy water, rinse and boil 15 minutes in water to cover. Turn off heat and leave jars and closures in the water until ready to fill.

Canning Tip: Always fill jars one at a time and seal each as soon as it is filled.

CANNY WAYS TO SPEED UP CANNING

Make Your Own Sterilizer:
A roasting pan doubles nicely as a sterilizer at canning time. Place clean jars in pan with water to cover; boil 15 minutes. Turn off heat; let jars stand in water until you're ready to fill them. Another tip: Before you start, check the tops of jars for any nicks or sharp edges.

Save Time, Save Work:
A ladle and a wide-neck funnel step up the job of filling jars, cut down on spills and cleanup. Large measuring cups and a colander are also helps in streamlining fixing.

Give Lids Special Care:
Use your kitchen tongs as your handy helper for lifting lids and rings from hot water. As a general rule, lids need scalding only—not boiling. But as there are several different kinds, it's good practice to follow manufacturer's directions for sterilizing.

Remove Air:
After filling each jar, take out the air bubbles by running a knife or narrow spatula around inside of jar. Add more liquid, if needed, to refill the jar to the rim. If left in, the air may cause the food to discolor.

Finish the Job—Right!

Large fruits such as pears or peaches fit neatly into a jar—even a small one—this way: Hold pieces, one at a time, on a fork and put in place, hollow side down and overlapping. A plate under the jar catches any drips.

Wipe the neck of each jar with a damp cloth before sealing, and cap. Let filled jars cool in a draft-free spot for about 12 hours, then label, date and store in a cool, dry, dark place.

TOMATOES, TOMATO SAUCES, MARMALADES AND PRESERVES

For each quart you will need about 3½ pounds of ripe tomatoes.
Twenty-five pounds are needed for a 7-quart sectioned water bath canner.

1 Fill colander or wire basket with tomatoes. Plunge into a large kettle of rapidly boiling water for 30 seconds to loosen skins. Plunge into cold water (fill sink or large dishpan). Remove skins and any green spots; core. Quarter or leave whole.
2 Pack firmly into clean hot quart jars, pressing down with a spoon until juice flows in spaces in jar. Fill to ½ inch of top. Add 1 teaspoon of salt to each jar. Wipe off top. Put on cover; tighten screw band.
3 Place jars in rack of water bath canner. Fill canner with hot water to 1 inch over tops of jars. Bring to boiling. Boil 45 minutes (sea level).
4 Remove from canner. Cool; test seal by pressing center of lid. If any jars have failed to seal, open, replace tops with new ones, then reprocess.

Old-Fashioned Chili Sauce
Makes 3 to 4 pints

16 cups chopped, peeled ripe tomatoes (about 6 pounds)
2 large onions, chopped (2 cups)
2 large red peppers, seeded and chopped (2 cups)
1 cup chopped celery
½ cup granulated sugar
½ cup firmly packed brown sugar
3 cups cider vinegar
3 tablespoons salt
1 tablespoon mustard seed
1 teaspoon whole allspice
1 teaspoon whole cloves
4 three-inch pieces stick cinnamon, broken

1 Combine tomatoes, onions, peppers, celery, sugar, vinegar and salt in a large kettle.
2 Tie mustard seed, allspice, cloves and cinnamon in several layers of cheesecloth. Add to kettle.
3 Heat to boiling; reduce heat; simmer, stirring occasionally, about 1¾ hours, or until thick. Discard spice bag.
4 Ladle into hot sterilized jars; seal, following manufacturer's directions. Label and date.

Barbecue Sauce

All-round sauce for franks, hamburgers, meat loaf, spareribs, pork chops.
Makes about 5 pints

15 ripe firm tomatoes
1 large onion, chopped
1 green pepper, chopped
4 cloves of garlic, minced
2 cups water
½ cup cider vinegar
½ cup Worcestershire sauce
½ cup brown sugar, firmly packed
4 teaspoons salt
4 teaspoons dry mustard
4 teaspoons chili powder
2 teaspoons celery salt
½ teaspoon liquid red pepper seasoning

1 Scald tomatoes in boiling water; dip in cold water; peel; cut in small pieces into large kettle; stir in remaining ingredients; heat to boiling.

1265

2 Simmer, stirring often, about 1 hour, or until sauce is about as thick as chili sauce.
3 Ladle into hot sterilized jars; seal.

Spiced Tomato Jam
Delicious with pork or ham as a spread for toast.
Makes about five 8-ounce jars

 6 ripe firm tomatoes
1½ teaspoons grated lemon peel
 2 teaspoons lemon juice
 ¼ teaspoon ground allspice
 ¼ teaspoon ground nutmeg
 1 package (about 2 ounces) powdered fruit
  pectin
 4 cups sugar

1 Scald tomatoes in boiling water; dip in cold water; peel; cut in small pieces into large kettle; stir in lemon peel and juice and spices; heat to boiling.
2 Add powdered fruit pectin, stirring constantly; stir in sugar; bring to full rolling boil; boil hard 1 minute; remove from heat.
3 Stir and skim top 5 minutes; ladle into hot sterilized jars; seal.

Dill Pear Tomatoes
Gourmet-seasoned appetizer or salad relish.
Makes about 6 pints

12 cups unripe (green) pear tomatoes*
 2 cloves of garlic, sliced
  Celery sticks
  Fresh dill sprigs with heads
 4 cups water
 2 cups cider vinegar
 ½ cup salt

1 Wash and stem tomatoes; pack into hot clean jars, each with 1 garlic slice, 1 celery stick and 1 dill head.
2 Boil water, vinegar, salt and dill sprigs 5 minutes in large saucepan; remove dill; fill jars; seal. Let season 4 to 6 weeks to blend seasonings.
*Or use tiny green regular tomatoes.

Tomato-Apple Chutney
It's peppery-hot! Serve with cold roast beef or pork for a flavor treat.
Makes one dozen 8-ounce jars or 6 pints

10 cups diced peeled ripe tomatoes (about 5 pounds)

 6 cups diced pared tart apples (about 3 pounds)
 2 large onions, chopped (2 cups)
 1 package (about 15 ounces) seedless raisins
 2 cloves garlic, minced
 1 pound dark brown sugar
 1 tablespoon salt
 2 teaspoons crushed dried hot red peppers
 1 tablespoon ground cinnamon
 1 teaspoon ground allspice
 ½ teaspoon ground ginger
 ½ teaspoon ground cloves
 2 cups cider vinegar

1 Combine all ingredients in a kettle. Heat, stirring constantly, to boiling; cover. Simmer 10 minutes; uncover. Simmer, stirring often, 30 minutes longer, or until thick.
2 Ladle into hot sterilized jars; seal, following manufacturer's directions. Cool jars, label and date.

Old-Fashioned Tomato Preserves
Makes five 8-ounce jars

 6 medium-size firm ripe tomatoes, peeled
 1 package (about 2 ounces) powdered fruit
  pectin
4½ cups sugar
 1 lemon, quartered and sliced thin

1 Place tomatoes in a large saucepan. (Do not add water or cover pan.) Heat to boiling; simmer 10 minutes.
2 Measure tomatoes, then return 3 cupfuls to pan; stir in pectin. Heat quickly, stirring several times, to boiling. Stir in sugar and lemon; heat again, stirring constantly, to boiling; cook 1 minute.
3 Ladle into hot sterilized jars; seal, following manufacturer's directions. Cool; label; date. Store in a cool, dry place.
Note—If using fancy containers, sterilize them first, then fill with preserves and top with a thin layer of melted paraffin. Cool completely and cap. If making preserves to give away within two weeks, simply store, covered, in the refrigerator, then ladle into containers of your choice.

Tomato and Pear Marmalade
Makes six 8-ounce jars

1½ pounds tomatoes
 1 pound pears
 ¼ cup lemon juice

1266

2 teaspoons grated lemon peel
1½ inches stick cinnamon
1 package (about 2 ounces) powdered fruit
   pectin
5 cups sugar

1 Place tomatoes in scalding water for 30 seconds; peel and cut into eighths; place in a medium-size saucepan. Bring to a boil; reduce heat; simmer 10 minutes; measure 2¼ cups.
2 Pare, core and dice pears to measure 2 cups. Toss pears with lemon juice and peel in a small bowl.
3 Combine tomatoes, pears, cinnamon stick and pectin in a kettle. Bring quickly to a boil, stirring occasionally. Add sugar; bring to a full rolling boil; boil rapidly 1 minute.
4 Remove from heat; skim off foam. Discard cinnamon stick. Stir and skim for 7 minutes to cool and prevent floating fruit; ladle into hot sterilized jars; seal, following manufacturer's directions. Label and date.

PICKLES, RELISHES AND CHUTNEYS

Spiced Cantaloupe Pickle

It's an ideal way to "save" some of summer's best melon to enjoy when the snow flies.
Makes 3 pints

2 large cantaloupes
3 cups sugar
1 lemon, sliced thin
1 tablespoon whole cloves
1 tablespoon whole allspice
6 one-inch sticks of cinnamon
1 teaspoon salt
1½ cups cider vinegar
1½ cups water

1 Quarter, seed and pare cantaloupes; cut meat into 1-inch cubes. (There should be about 8 cups.)
2 Combine cantaloupe with remaining ingredients in a kettle; heat to boiling. Simmer, stirring often from bottom of kettle, 45 minutes, or until melon is translucent and syrup is slightly thickened.
3 Ladle into hot sterilized jars; fill with remaining hot syrup. Seal, following manufacturer's directions.
4 Let jars cool; label; store in a cool dry place.

Watermelon Rind Pickle
Makes six 8-ounce jars

Rind from half of a large watermelon (about 2 pounds)
8 cups water (for brine)
½ cup salt
4 cups sugar
1 lemon, thinly sliced
1 tablespoon whole cloves
1 tablespoon whole allspice
6 one-inch sticks of cinnamon
2 cups cider vinegar
2 cups water (for syrup)

1 Pare green skin from watermelon; cut rind into 1-inch cubes. (There should be about 8 cups.) Soak overnight in brine of 8 cups water and salt in large bowl.
2 Drain; place in kettle; cover with fresh water. Heat to boiling, then simmer 10 minutes, or just until cubes are tender but still firm; drain.
3 While rind drains, combine sugar, lemon, cloves, allspice, cinnamon, vinegar and 2 cups water in same kettle; heat to boiling; stir in drained rind. Simmer, stirring often from bottom of pan, 1 hour, or until rind is clear and syrup is thick.
4 Ladle rind and spice evenly into hot sterilized jars; fill to brim with remaining hot syrup. Seal, following manufacturer's directions. Label and store in a cool dry place.

Green Tomato Chowchow

Lucky you, if you have a garden: Here's a very special way to use last-of-the-season tomatoes.
Makes about three pints

2 pounds green tomatoes, cored and
   chopped (about 8 cups)
4 large onions, chopped (4 cups)
1 cup sugar
1½ teaspoons salt
1 teaspoon dry mustard
½ teaspoon pepper
½ teaspoon ground allspice
½ teaspoon ground cloves
2 cups cider vinegar

1 Combine all ingredients in a kettle. Heat slowly, stirring often, to boiling. Simmer, stirring often from bottom of kettle, 45 minutes, or until thickened and translucent.

1267

2 Ladle into hot sterilized jars; seal, following manufacturer's directions.
3 Let jars cool; label; store in a cool dry place.

Dilled Zucchini
They taste a bit like cucumber pickles, but what a delightful change!
Makes a dozen 8-ounce jars or 6 pints

6 pounds zucchini, trimmed and sliced thin (about 16 cups)
2 cups thinly sliced celery
2 large onions, chopped (2 cups)
⅓ cup salt
Ice cubes
2 cups sugar
2 tablespoons dill seeds
2 cups white vinegar
6 cloves garlic, halved

1 Mix zucchini, celery, onions and salt in a large bowl; place a layer of ice cubes on top; cover. Let stand 3 hours; drain well.
2 Combine sugar, dill seeds and vinegar in a kettle; heat, stirring constantly, to boiling; stir in vegetables. Heat, stirring several times, *just* to a full rolling boil.
3 Ladle into hot sterilized jars; place 1 or 2 pieces garlic in each. Seal, following manufacturer's directions. Cool jars, label and date.

Pickled Eggplant
Makes 3 to 4 pints

2 pounds eggplant, trimmed and cut into 1-inch cubes (8 cups)
1 cup thinly sliced celery
1 large onion, thinly sliced
1 green pepper, seeded and cut into strips
1 red pepper, seeded and cut into strips
⅓ cup salt
Ice cubes
1½ cups sugar
1 tablespoon dill seeds
1½ cups cider vinegar
4 cloves of garlic, halved

1 Combine eggplant, celery, onion, green pepper, red pepper and salt in a large bowl; place a layer of ice cubes on top; cover. Let stand for 3 hours; drain well.
2 Combine sugar, dill seeds and vinegar in a kettle or large saucepan; bring to boiling, stirring constantly; stir in vegetables. Bring to boiling again, stirring occasionally; remove from heat.

1268

3 Ladle into hot sterilized jars; place 1 or 2 pieces of garlic in each jar. Seal, following manufacturer's directions. Label and date.

Dilled Carrot Sticks
They're sharply seasoned, with a subtle flavor of dill. Try them as a dinner pickle—or even an appetizer snack.
Makes 4 pints

2 pounds carrots (about 20 medium-size)
½ cup chopped fresh dill
2 cloves of garlic, peeled and halved
2 cups water
2 cups white vinegar
4 tablespoons salt
4 tablespoons sugar
½ teaspoon cayenne

1 Pare carrots and cut into about-4-inch-long sticks. Cook, covered, in boiling unsalted water in a kettle 5 minutes, or just until crisply tender.
2 Lift out with slotted spoon; place at once in a large bowl of ice and water to cool quickly.
3 Pack carrot sticks upright in hot sterilized jars; place 2 tablespoons dill and ½ clove of garlic in each.
4 Heat water, vinegar, salt, sugar and cayenne to boiling in a medium-size saucepan; pour into jars to fill. Seal, following manufacturer's directions.
5 Let jars cool; label; store in a cool dry place.

Calico Carrot Chop-Chop
Try some now on those last-of-the-barbecue-season hot dogs or hamburgers.
Makes a dozen 8-ounce jars or 6 pints

20 medium-size carrots, pared and cut up
4 large sweet green peppers, quartered and seeded
4 large sweet red peppers, quartered and seeded
6 large onions, peeled and quartered
2 cups sugar
2 tablespoons salt
1 tablespoon dry mustard
2 cups cider vinegar

1 Put carrots, green and red peppers and onions through a food chopper, using a coarse blade. (There should be about 14 cups.)
2 Place in a kettle; add boiling water to cover; let stand 5 minutes, then drain well. Return vegetables to kettle.
3 Stir in remaining ingredients. Heat, stirring several times, to boiling, then simmer, stirring once or twice, 5 minutes.

Pickles all-of-a-kind and pickles mixed, pickles big and pickles little, pickles sweet and sour, pickle relishes, catsups, conserves and chutneys. All recipes—more, too—are included.

4 Ladle into hot sterilized jars; seal, following manufacturer's directions. Cool jars, label and date.

Fiesta Corn Relish
Limas blend with the corn for this mild sweet-sour mealtime extra.
Makes a dozen 8-ounce jars or 6 pints

   12 medium-size ears of corn

   4 cups shelled fresh lima beans (about 4 pounds)
   1 cup thinly sliced celery
   1 large onion, chopped (1 cup)
   ½ cup chopped sweet red pepper
   ½ cup chopped sweet green pepper
  1½ cups sugar
   2 tablespoons mustard seed
   4 teaspoons salt
   3 cups white vinegar
   3 cups water

1 Peel husks and silks from corn. Place ears in a kettle; pour in boiling water to cover. Heat to boiling again; cook 5 minutes; drain. Cool until easy to handle, then cut corn from cobs. (There should be 8 cups.)

2 Combine corn with remaining ingredients in a kettle; heat, stirring several times, to boiling. Cook, uncovered, 20 minutes.

3 Ladle into hot sterilized jars; seal, following manufacturer's directions. Cool jars, label and date.

New England Corn Relish
Makes six 8-ounce jars

  1 cup sugar
  ¼ cup sifted all-purpose flour
1½ teaspoons turmeric
  1 teaspoon salt
  2 cups cider vinegar
  2 cans (12 or 16 ounces) whole-kernel corn, drained
  2 cups finely shredded cabbage
  2 medium-size sweet red peppers, quartered, seeded and chopped

1 Combine sugar, flour, turmeric and salt in a kettle; stir in vinegar and vegetables.

2 Heat slowly to boiling; cook, stirring often, 10 minutes, or until mixture thickens.

3 Ladle into hot sterilized jars; seal, following manufacturer's directions. Cool; store.

Coleslaw Relish
Cabbage stays refreshingly crisp and has a tart, tangy flavor.
Makes a dozen 8-ounce jars or 6 pints

16 cups finely shredded green cabbage (about 4 pounds)
  4 cups chopped onions (4 large)
  1 cup diced sweet green pepper
  1 cup diced sweet red pepper
  ⅔ cup salt
  2 cups sugar
  1 teaspoon celery seed
  2 cups white vinegar

1 Mix cabbage, onions, green and red peppers and salt in a large bowl. Pour in ice water to cover; cover. Let stand overnight.

2 Drain vegetables well; pack into hot sterilized jars.

3 Combine sugar, celery seed and vinegar in

a medium-size saucepan; heat, stirring constantly, to boiling.

4 Pour into jars to fill to rim; seal, following manufacturer's directions. Cool jars, label and date.

Cucumber Relish Compote
Chunks of cucumber, onion, and oranges make this unusual, so-good combination.
Makes eighteen 8-ounce jars or 9 pints

  9 large cucumbers
30 small white onions, peeled
  ¼ cup salt
  2 large seedless oranges
  3 cups sugar
  3 cups white vinegar
  2 teaspoons whole cloves

1 Quarter cucumbers lengthwise; cut into 1-inch pieces. (There should be about 16 cups.) Halve onions; combine with cucumbers and salt in a large bowl; let stand 1 hour; drain.

2 Slice oranges ¼ inch thick; quarter each. Place in a small bowl; cover with boiling water; let stand 1 hour; drain.

3 Combine sugar and vinegar in a kettle; heat, stirring constantly, to boiling. Stir in vegetables and oranges; cover. Heat *just* to a full rolling boil.

4 Ladle into hot sterilized jars, placing 5 or 6 whole cloves in each; seal, following manufacturer's directions. Cool jars, label and date.

Red Pepper Relish
Makes six 8-ounce jars

10 medium-size carrots, pared and coarsely chopped
  4 large sweet red peppers, quartered and seeded
  3 large onions, peeled and quartered
  1 cup sugar
  1 tablespoon salt
  1 teaspoon dry mustard
  1 cup cider vinegar

1 Put carrots, red peppers and onions through a food chopper, using a coarse blade. (There should be about 7 cups.)

2 Place in a kettle; add boiling water to cover; let stand 5 minutes; drain thoroughly. Return vegetables to kettle.

3 Stir in sugar, salt, mustard and vinegar. Bring

to boil, stirring occasionally. Reduce heat; simmer, stirring once or twice, 5 minutes.

4 Ladle into hot sterilized jars; seal, following manufacturer's directions. Cool jars; label and date.

Relish-Stuffed Peppers
Makes 5 or 6 one-and-one-half pints

6 red peppers
6 green peppers
6 cups finely shredded green cabbage
2 cups thinly sliced carrots
1 cup salt
4 quarts water
2 tablespoons mustard seed
1 tablespoon celery seeds
2 quarts white vinegar
3 cups sugar

1 Cut stem ends from peppers and reserve. Remove seeds and white membranes from peppers.
2 Combine cabbage and carrots in a large bowl or kettle (not aluminum). Place the peppers and their stem ends on top. Dissolve salt in water; pour over vegetables to cover; let stand in cool place 24 hours. Drain; rinse in cold water and drain thoroughly.
3 Combine cabbage and carrot mixture, mustard seed and celery seed in a large bowl; toss to mix well; fill peppers, dividing mixture evenly; replace stem ends.
4 Pack stuffed peppers into sterilized jars, mixing red and green.
5 In large saucepan, combine vinegar and sugar; bring to a full rolling boil, stirring occasionally. Pour boiling hot liquid over peppers in jars, leaving ½-inch space on top. Seal, following manufacturer's directions. Label and date.

Calico Pepper Relish
So good, and easy, you'll wish you'd made more. Serve some right now on those outdoor-cooked hamburgers.
Makes 4 pints

1 pound carrots, pared (about 10 medium-size)
4 large green peppers, quartered and seeded
4 large red peppers, quartered and seeded
4 large onions, peeled and quartered
1½ cups sugar

2 tablespoons salt
1½ cups cider vinegar

1 Put carrots, green and red peppers and onions through food chopper, using coarse blade. (There should be about 10 cups when ground, so use a large shallow pan or dish to catch them.)
2 Cover vegetables with boiling water in a kettle; let stand 5 minutes; drain well.
3 Return vegetables to kettle; stir in sugar, salt and vinegar; heat to boiling. Simmer, stirring once or twice, 5 minutes.
4 Ladle into hot sterilized jars; seal, following manufacturer's directions.
5 Let jars cool; label; store in a cool dry place.

Pungent Cucumber Relish
Makes 6 pints

3 pounds cucumbers, pared and chopped (8 cups)
1 large onion, chopped (1 cup)
2 large red peppers, seeded and chopped (2 cups)
2 large green peppers, seeded and chopped (2 cups)
1 tablespoon ground turmeric
½ cup coarse or kosher salt
Water
2 tablespoons mixed pickling spices
2 three-inch pieces stick cinnamon, broken
4 cups cider vinegar
2 cups firmly packed brown sugar

1 Combine cucumbers, onions, red and green peppers, turmeric and salt in a large kettle.
2 Add water just to cover (about 8 cups); let stand 3 to 4 hours; drain. Cover vegetables again with water; let stand 1 hour; drain.
3 Tie pickling spices and cinnamon in several layers of cheesecloth. Place in a medium-size saucepan with vinegar and brown sugar. Heat to boiling; pour over drained vegetables in kettle.
4 Cover; let stand 12 to 18 hours at room temperature. Next day bring mixture to boiling. Discard spice bag.
5 Ladle into hot sterilized jars; seal, following manufacturer's directions. Label and date.

1271

Dilled Appetizer Relish
Serve these sweet-sour fancies with tomato juice or as a dinner extra.
Makes 2 pints

2 cans (3 or 4 ounces each) mushroom caps
1⅓ cups pitted ripe olives
⅔ cup stuffed green olives
1 pimiento, cut into ¼-inch-wide strips
1 small onion, peeled and sliced
¾ cup white vinegar
⅓ cup sugar
1 teaspoon dillweed

1 Drain mushrooms, saving ⅓ cup of the liquid for next step. Layer mushrooms with olives and pimiento into hot sterilized wide-mouth jars to make a pretty pattern. Place onion slices on top.
2 Heat vinegar with the ⅓ cup mushroom liquid, sugar and dillweed to boiling in a small saucepan; pour over vegetables in jars to fill to top.
3 Cap and seal, following manufacturer's directions, and store in the refrigerator. Plan to use within 4 weeks.

Crispy Harvest Relish

A sweet-sour flavor blend that goes with most everything.
Makes about 8 pints

24 green tomatoes
6 cups finely shredded green cabbage
3 cups chopped onions
1 cup diced celery
2 green peppers, diced
1 cup salt
3 cups cider vinegar
1 cup water
2 cups granulated sugar
2 cups brown sugar, firmly packed
2 tablespoons celery seed
2 tablespoons mustard seed

1 Wash and stem tomatoes; cut into *very thin* slices; measure (there should be about 5 quarts).
2 Sprinkle layers of tomatoes, cabbage, onions, celery and peppers with salt in bowl; let stand overnight.
3 Next day, drain vegetables well; place in kettle.
4 Heat remaining ingredients to boiling in large saucepan; pour over vegetables; cover kettle; cook over medium heat, stirring often, 15 to 20 minutes, or just until vegetables are crispy tender. *Do not overcook.*
5 Pack into hot sterilized jars; seal.

Pennsylvania Dutch Chowchow
Makes 8 pints

2 packages (10 ounces each) frozen lima beans

1272

1 package (10 ounces) frozen cut green beans
2 cups thinly sliced pared carrots
20 small white onions, peeled and halved
1 package (10 ounces) frozen whole-kernel corn
2 cups small cauliflowerets
3 cups sliced pared cucumbers
2 cups thinly sliced celery
1 large green pepper, halved, seeded and diced (1 cup)
1 large red pepper, halved, seeded and diced (1 cup)
2 cups sugar
1 tablespoon salt
1 tablespoon mustard seed
3 cups white vinegar
1 cup water

1 Cook lima beans, green beans and carrots in lightly salted boiling water in separate medium-size saucepans 3 minutes, or just until crisply tender; drain. Combine all with onions in a roasting pan.
2 Cook corn and cauliflowerets in lightly salted boiling water in separate medium-size saucepans 1 minute; drain. Add to other vegetables with cucumbers, celery and peppers.
3 Sprinkle sugar, salt and mustard seed over vegetables; drizzle with vinegar and water; mix lightly.
4 Measure 4 cups of the vegetable mixture and 1 cup of the liquid into a medium-size saucepan; heat to a full rolling boil; spoon into 2 sterilized pint jars. Seal, following manufacturer's directions.
5 Repeat heating and filling jars with remaining vegetable mixture and liquid, heating only 4 cups at a time to avoid overcooking. Cool jars; label; date.

Chowchow Pickle
Makes 5 pints

1 medium-size head cauliflower
2 cups thinly sliced carrots (3 large)
12 small white onions
3 large cucumbers
2 large green peppers
2 large red peppers
2 cups thinly sliced celery
3 cups white vinegar
1 cup water
2 cups sugar
1 tablespoon salt
1 tablespoon mustard seed
2 teaspoons curry powder

1 Wash cauliflower; trim off leaves and core; separate into tiny flowerets (you should have

The prettiest pantry shelf is one laden with pickles you have put up.

about 5 cups). Cook in salted boiling water in a large saucepan for 1 minute; drain.

2 Cook carrots in salted boiling water in a large saucepan for 3 minutes; drain.

3 Pour boiling water over onions in a small bowl; let stand one minute; drain. Peel off skins; cut onions in half.

4 Pare cucumbers; cut in half; scoop out seeds. Cut into long strips, ¼-inch thick; cut strips into 1-inch lengths.

5 Cut green and red peppers in half; remove seeds; cut peppers into 1-inch pieces; combine with prepared cauliflower, carrots, onions, cucumbers and celery in a large kettle.

6 Combine vinegar, water, sugar, salt, mustard seed and curry powder in a medium-size bowl; stir until sugar is dissolved.

7 Pour vinegar mixture into kettle with vegetables. Heat to boiling.

8 Ladle into hot sterilized jars; seal, following manufacturer's directions. Label and date.

●

Cucumber Crisps
Overnight chilling in ice water keeps the cucumbers pleasingly crunchy.
Makes ten 8-ounce jars or 5 pints

8 cups thinly sliced unpared cucumbers (about 6 large)
8 cups thinly sliced peeled onions (about 16 medium-size)
½ cup salt
Dill sprigs
1 pound light brown sugar
¼ cup chopped fresh dill
2 cups white vinegar

1 Mix cucumbers, onions and salt in a large bowl; pour in ice water to cover; cover. Let stand overnight.
2 Drain vegetables well; pack into hot sterilized jars; place a small sprig of dill in each.
3 Heat brown sugar, chopped dill and vinegar, stirring constantly, to boiling in a medium-size saucepan; pour into jars to fill to rim. Seal, following manufacturer's directions. Cool jars, label and date.

Cucumber Conserve
Makes six 8-ounce jars

3 medium-size cucumbers, trimmed and sliced thin (4 cups)
½ cup golden raisins
¾ cup water
½ cup lime juice
1 package (about 2 ounces) powdered fruit pectin
5 cups sugar
Green food coloring

1 Combine cucumbers, raisins, water, lime juice and pectin in a kettle. Heat quickly, stirring often, to boiling.
2 Stir in sugar, then a few drops food coloring to tint pale green. Heat, stirring constantly, to a full rolling boil, then cook, stirring constantly, 1 minute; remove from heat.
3 Ladle into hot sterilized jars; seal following manufacturer's directions. Cool; label; date. Store in a cool, dry place.

1274

JAMS, JELLIES PRESERVES AND FRUIT CHUTNEYS

Ginger Pears
Fruit is easiest to handle if you cook it in small batches.
Makes 3 pints

12 medium-size firm ripe pears (about 4 pounds)
¼ cup sliced preserved or crystallized ginger
3 cups sugar
½ cup water
½ cup lemon juice

1 Cut pears in half; pare and core.
2 Combine ginger, sugar, water and lemon juice in a large frying pan; heat, stirring constantly, to boiling; add pears. Simmer 10 to 15 minutes, or until tender but still firm enough to hold their shape. Lift from syrup with a slotted spoon and pack into hot sterilized jars.
3 Cook syrup 15 minutes longer, or until reduced to about half the amount; pour over pears in jars to fill to rim. Seal, following manufacturer's directions. Cool jars, label and date.

Pear Conserve
Makes eight 8-ounce jars

2½ pounds ripe peaches, peeled, pitted and chopped (2 cups)
2½ pounds ripe pears, pared, cored and chopped (2 cups)
¼ cup lemon juice
7½ cups sugar
½ bottle liquid fruit pectin (from a 6-ounce bottle)
½ cup drained maraschino cherries, quartered
½ cup blanched slivered almonds

1 Combine peaches, pears and lemon juice in a large kettle; stir in sugar.
2 Place over high heat; bring to a full rolling boil and boil hard, stirring constantly, 1 minute.
3 Remove from heat; stir in liquid pectin all at once, stirring and skimming for 5 minutes. Stir in cherries and almonds.
4 Ladle into hot sterilized jars or glasses; seal, following manufacturer's directions. Label and date.

Anise Pear Relish
Makes 4 generous servings

1 can (1 pound) pear halves
1 tablespoon lemon juice
1 teaspoon grated lemon rind
1 teaspoon aniseseed

1 Drain pear syrup into a 1-cup measure; add water, if needed, to make 1 cup. Place pears in a medium-size bowl.

2 Combine syrup with lemon juice, lemon rind and aniseed in a small saucepan. Heat to boiling, then simmer 15 minutes; pour over pears.

3 Chill in the refrigerator for several hours to season and blend flavors. Serve the relish with roast pork, baked ham, or roast veal.

Pear Honey
Makes six 8-ounce jars

6 large ripe pears, pared and cored
1 lemon, thinly sliced
5 cups sugar

1 Put pears through a food chopper, using the fine blade. (There should be about 4 cups.)

2 Combine with lemon and sugar in a large kettle. Bring to boiling, stirring constantly. Reduce heat; simmer, stirring occasionally, until mixture is thickened and clear, about 30 minutes.

3 Ladle into hot sterilized jars or glasses; seal, following manufacturer's directions. Label and date.

Peach Chutney
Makes 1¾ cups

1 can (1 pound) cling-peach slices
1 large onion, chopped (1 cup)
½ cup seedless raisins
1 clove garlic, minced
¼ cup firmly packed brown sugar
½ teaspoon salt
¼ cup cider vinegar
¼ teaspoon liquid red pepper seasoning

1 In a medium-size saucepan, combine peach slices and syrup with remaining ingredients.

2 Heat to boiling, then simmer, stirring often, 20 minutes, or until thickened; pour into a medium-size bowl. Cool, then chill several hours to blend flavors. Serve with a curry or with roast pork.

Spiced Peach Spiral
Makes 2 pints

1 can (1 pound, 13 ounces) cling peach halves
2 tablespoons honey
2 tablespoons lemon juice
1 one-inch piece of stick cinnamon

1 lemon
8 whole cloves

1 Drain syrup from peaches into a small saucepan; stir in honey and lemon juice; add cinnamon stick. Heat to boiling; simmer 10 minutes; remove from heat. Take out cinnamon stick.

2 Cut rind from lemon in one long strip about ¼ inch wide; stud with whole cloves.

3 Place peaches, rounded sides down, and lemon spiral, in hot sterilized jars just wide enough to hold a peach half.

4 Pour hot syrup over; seal, following manufacturer's directions; cool completely. Or use a sterilized fancy container, and, after filling, top with a thin layer of melted paraffin; cool completely; cap. Store sterilized jars in the refrigerator. Plan to use within 4 weeks.

Brandied Peaches
Makes six 8-ounce jars

3 pounds small ripe freestone peaches
2 cups sugar
2 cups water
6 whole cloves
12 tablespoons apricot brandy

1 Dip peaches into boiling water for 30 seconds; peel, halve and pit.

2 Combine sugar, water and cloves in a medium-size saucepan; heat to boiling; simmer 5 minutes.

3 Add half the peaches to the syrup; simmer 5 minutes; remove, with a slotted spoon, to 3 of the hot sterilized jars; cover loosely. Repeat with remaining peaches and jars. Boil syrup to reduce volume to about 1½ cups.

4 Add 2 tablespoons brandy to each jar of peaches. Spoon in syrup, discarding cloves, and filling jars to within ½ inch of top, holding peaches with a fork to allow any air bubbles to rise to top. Seal, following manufacturer's directions. Cool jars; label and date.

1275

Raspberry-Peach Conserve
Makes eight 8-ounce jars

1½ pounds ripe peaches
2 cups fresh raspberries
1 cup raisins
2 tablespoons lemon juice
1 package (about 2 ounces) powdered fruit pectin
7 cups sugar
½ cup coarsely chopped walnuts

1 Dip peaches into boiling water for 30 seconds; peel, halve, pit and chop.

2 Combine peaches, raspberries, raisins, lemon juice and pectin in a large kettle. Bring quickly to boiling, stirring occasionally. Add sugar; bring again to a full rolling boil; boil rapidly 1 minute. Remove from heat; skim off foam. Add walnuts.

3 Stir and skim for 7 minutes to cool and prevent floating fruit.

4 Ladle into hot sterilized jars or glasses; seal, following manufacturer's directions. Label and date.

Strawberry-Apricot Preserves
Makes six 8-ounce jars

4 cups (2 pints) strawberries, washed and hulled
4 cups sugar
1 package (about 2 ounces) powdered fruit pectin
1 can (6 ounces) apricot nectar

1 Crush strawberries, a layer at a time, in a large bowl; measure. (There should be 2 cups.)

2 Stir in sugar; let stand, stirring occasionally, until sugar is dissolved, about 15 minutes.

3 Heat pectin and apricot nectar to boiling in a small saucepan; boil hard, stirring constantly, 1 minute; stir into fruit and continue stirring 3 minutes. (Some sugar crystals will remain.)

4 Ladle quickly into hot sterilized jars or freezer containers; cover tightly. Let stand 24 hours at room temperature; label and date. Store in freezer. (If preserves are to be eaten within 2 or 3 weeks, store in refrigerator.)

No-Cook Apricot Marmalade
Makes three 8-ounce jars

1 package (8 ounces) dried apricots (about 2 cups)
1 cup water
½ cup orange juice
¼ cup lemon juice
1 teaspoon grated lemon peel
2 cups sugar

1 Soak apricots overnight in water in a large bowl. Lift out with a slotted spoon, letting liquid drain back into bowl. Put apricots through a food chopper, using fine blade.

2 Stir orange and lemon juices into liquid in bowl; stir in apricots, lemon peel and sugar. (Sugar will dissolve as mixture stands.)

3 Spoon into hot sterilized jars or fancy containers; top with a thin layer of melted paraffin; cool slightly; cap. Store in the refrigerator. Plan to use within 4 weeks.

Strawberry-Pineapple Preserves
Makes about five 8-ounce jars

1 bag (about 1¼ pounds) frozen unsweetened whole strawberries (about 4 cups)
1 can (about 14 ounces) crushed pineapple
3½ cups sugar

1 Combine strawberries, pineapple and syrup and sugar in a large heavy saucepan. (No need to thaw berries.) Heat, stirring often, until sugar dissolves and mixture comes to a boil.

2 Cook, stirring often, until syrup registers 220° on a candy thermometer. (Syrup will fall slowly off a spoon in two drops that run together.)

3 Spoon into hot sterilized jars and seal, following manufacturer's directions; cool completely. Or use a sterilized fancy container, and, after filling, top with a thin layer of melted paraffin; cool completely; cap. Store in cool, dry place.

Pineapple-Orange Wine Jelly
Makes four 6-ounce glasses

3¼ cups sugar
1¼ cups white wine
½ bottle liquid fruit pectin (from a 6-ounce bottle)
1 can (6 ounces) frozen concentrated pineapple-orange juice, thawed

1 Combine sugar and wine in a large saucepan.

2 Bring quickly to a full rolling boil, stirring constantly; boil hard 1 minute.

3 Remove from heat; stir in liquid fruit pectin and thawed juice. Mix well.

4 Ladle jelly quickly into hot sterilized jelly glasses; top each with a thin layer of melted paraffin. Cool jars; cap, label and date.

Sweet Pepper-and-Orange Jam
Makes seven 8-ounce jars

25 sweet red peppers (about 6 pounds)
1 large seedless orange, peeled and cut into pieces
2 cups cider vinegar

1276

4½ cups sugar
1 teaspoon salt

1 Wash peppers; cut in half; remove seeds and white membrane; cut into large pieces; put through food chopper using coarsest blade.
2 Drain peppers well and discard liquid. Grind orange.
3 Combine chopped peppers, orange, vinegar, sugar and salt in a large kettle. Bring quickly to boiling, stirring constantly. Cook over high heat, stirring often, about 30 minutes, or just until mixture is thick and clear like jam. (Do not overcook.)
4 Ladle into hot sterilized jars or glasses; seal, following manufacturer's directions. Label and date.

Sour Cherry Conserve
Makes eight 8-ounce jars

3 pounds sour cherries, stemmed and pitted
  (3 cups)
1 can (about 9 ounces) crushed pineapple
½ cup raisins
7 cups sugar
1 bottle (6 ounces) liquid fruit pectin
1 cup coarsely chopped walnuts

1 Combine sour cherries, crushed pineapple, raisins and sugar in a large kettle.
2 Bring quickly to a full rolling boil, stirring constantly; then boil hard for 1 minute.
3 Remove from heat; stir in liquid fruit pectin. Mix well; skim off foam. Add walnuts.
4 Stir and skim for 7 minutes to cool and prevent floating fruit. Ladle into hot sterilized jars or glasses; seal, following manufacturer's directions. Label and date.

Sweet-Sour Cherries
Makes about four 8-ounce jars

4 cups red tart cherries, washed, stemmed and
  pitted
2 cups cider vinegar
4 cups sugar

1 Cover cherries with vinegar in large bowl; let stand overnight. In the morning turn into sieve; let drain thoroughly about 2 hours.
2 Return drained cherries to large bowl; stir in sugar; cover; set aside in a cool place (not refrigerator).

3 Stir mixture every day for about 10 days, or until all the sugar has dissolved.
4 Ladle mixture into hot sterilized jars; seal; wipe; label; store in a cool dry place.

Plum Catsup
Makes five 8-ounce jars

4 pounds purple plums
1 large onion, chopped (1 cup)
¾ cup water
3½ cups sugar
1¼ cups cider vinegar
1 clove of garlic, peeled
1 teaspoon salt
½ teaspoon ground cinnamon
⅛ teaspoon liquid red pepper seasoning
⅓ cup mixed pickling spices

1 Wash plums; cut in half; remove and discard pits. Combine plums with onion and water in a large kettle. Bring to boiling; reduce heat; cover; simmer until plums are very soft, about 30 minutes.
2 Press plum mixture through a fine sieve or food mill into a large bowl. Return plum puree to large kettle; stir in sugar, vinegar, garlic, salt, cinnamon and red pepper seasoning.
3 Tie pickling spices in several layers of cheesecloth; add to kettle.
4 Bring mixture to boiling; reduce heat; simmer, stirring frequently, 30 minutes, or until catsup is very thick. Remove and discard garlic and spice bag.
5 Ladle into hot sterilized jars; seal, following manufacturer's directions. Label and date.

Parslied Apple Jelly
Makes six 8-ounce jars

1277

8 pounds tart cooking apples, washed
8 cups water
4½ cups sugar
⅔ cup white vinegar
1 cup chopped parsley
  Several drops green food coloring

1 Remove stem and blossom ends of apples; do not pare or core; slice or chop. Combine with water in a very large kettle.* Bring to boiling; reduce heat; cover. Simmer 20 minutes, or until apples are soft.

2 Pour cooked apple mixture into a damp jelly bag. (Make your own from unbleached muslin or several thicknesses of cheesecloth.) Let stand without squeezing for at least 4 hours, or until clear liquid has stopped dripping out. (Or pour apple mixture through several layers of wet cheesecloth in a colander placed over a large bowl.) You will get about 4 cups.

3 Combine apple juice with sugar and vinegar in a large kettle; bring to a full rolling boil; continue to boil for about 20 minutes, stirring and skimming occasionally, or until mixture registers 220° on a candy thermometer at sea level. (For higher elevations use temperature 8° higher than temperature at which water boils.) If you do not have a thermometer, test with clean metal spoon; jelly is done when the drops run together and fall off the spoon in a sheet or flake.

4 When jelly is done, remove from heat; stir in parsley and a few drops of food coloring to tint a pleasing green. Continue to skim and stir for 7 minutes.

5 Ladle into hot sterilized jars or glasses; seal, following manufacturer's directions. Label and date.

*If you do not have a very large kettle, divide recipe in half; prepare one half at a time.

Cranberry Catsup
Makes four 8-ounce jars

2 packages (1 pound each) cranberries
1 large onion, chopped (1 cup)
1¼ cups water
2 cups sugar
2 teaspoons salt
1½ teaspoons ground cinnamon
1 teaspoon ground cloves
1 teaspoon ground allspice
½ teaspoon pepper
1 cup cider vinegar

1 Combine cranberries, onion and water in a large kettle. Bring to boiling; reduce heat; cover; simmer until cranberries are tender, about 20 minutes. Press through a fine sieve or food mill.

2 Return cranberry puree to kettle; stir in sugar, salt, cinnamon, cloves, allspice, pepper and vinegar. Simmer, uncovered, stirring constantly, 5 minutes, or until catsup is very thick.

3 Ladle into hot sterilized jars; seal, following manufacturer's directions. Label and date.

Spicy Cranberry Chutney
Makes four 8-ounce jars

4 cups (1 pound) fresh cranberries
1 cup seedless raisins
1⅔ cups sugar
1 tablespoon ground cinnamon
1½ teaspoons ground ginger
¼ teaspoon ground cloves
1 cup water
1 medium-size onion, peeled and chopped
1 medium-size apple, pared, quartered, cored and chopped
½ cup thinly sliced celery

1 Combine cranberries, raisins, sugar, spices and water in a large saucepan. Simmer 15 minutes, or until berries pop and mixture thickens.

2 Stir in onion, apple and celery; simmer 15 minutes longer, or until mixture is thick.

3 Ladle into hot sterilized jars; seal, following manufacturer's directions.

INDEX TO RECIPES IN THIS VOLUME

1280